Soul
PROOF

Compelling evidence we are immortal
spiritual beings—and what that means for our lives!

by Dr. Mark Pitstick

All inquiries should be addressed to
Mark R. Pitstick, MA, DC;
P.O Box 1604, Chillicothe, OH 45601.

Soul Proof:
Compelling Evidence We Are Immortal Spiritual Beings
by Dr. Mark R. Pitstick $19.95   ISBN 0-9661419-6-2

Warning/Disclaimer

Every effort has been made to make this collection of materials as complete and accurate as possible. Nevertheless, information may change, and there may be mistakes, both typographical and in content. Important data may be omitted. Therefore, this book should be used as a general guide only and not as a final source of information.

Further, all statements made by the author, Dr. Mark R. Pitstick, are based on his own personal research and study; they do not necessarily reflect the beliefs of all professionals. It should also be noted that in no way is any information contained herein meant to take the place of or to provide any kind of professional advice or treatment, nor does it preclude the need to seek the advice of professionals on a personal level.

Acknowledgements

To my beloved family and friends for all your love, support, and assistance.

To Bernie Siegel, M.D., for writing the foreword. To Ken Ring, Ph.D., Wayne Dyer, Ed.D., Neil Douglas-Klotz, Ph.D., Michael Newton, Ph.D., Jeffrey Mishlove, Ph.D., and Walter Semkiw, M.D., for their exclusive contributions to the book.

To Raymond Moody, Ph.D., M.D., for his valuable contributions to the book and for training me in the facilitated ADC technique. To Brian Weiss, M.D., for sharing invaluable insights during our radio interview and for training me in past life regression therapy.

To Wendy Keller, Dr. Paul Brown, Lainey Ebright, and Otto and Susie Collins for their editorial assistance.

To Tobi Flynn and Ryan Roghaar for their wonderful interior and cover design work.

To Chuck and Cheryl Beckert for the cover graphic and other help.

To the many researchers, teachers, and explorers whose findings I have quoted.

To all those who have struggled to find sensible answers to their questions about God, afterlife, and soul issues. May you deeply know how very much God and the Heavenly Host cares for, guides, and assists us.

Finally, to Great Spirit/Universe/Self for more fully revealing Its wondrous nature as the ultimate love, joy, peace, wisdom, and beauty throughout eternity.

TABLE OF CONTENTS

∞ FOREWORD ∞

by Bernie Siegel, M.D.

I am a believer in the reality of afterlife and our spiritual natures not because of other people's stories or beliefs but because my personal and professional life experiences have convinced me. As such, I am pleased and honored to write a foreword for *Soul Proof: Compelling Evidence We Are Immortal Spiritual Beings*. Mark has assembled a wealth of evidence including firsthand, religious, and clinical indications that can be immensely comforting and healing if you are open minded and ready to believe.

As a four-year-old, I almost choked to death when I took a toy apart and put the pieces in my mouth as I had seen carpenters do. I accidentally aspirated them and was choking to death, a very unpleasant way to die, and was pleased when I left my body. I was at peace while looking down at my body, watching myself choking to death. Being out of my body was more interesting than being in it. I had no problem with dying but I was upset, as most children are who have this experience, that my parents would come in and find me dead. My feeling was, 'I prefer death, it is more interesting than being alive and in my body.'

So I can relate to those who are blind from birth and can see for the first time during their near-death or out-of-body experiences. They're also disappointed when they are resuscitated because now they're blind again. When you meet individuals who are born blind and have these experiences of seeing while out of their bodies, you have to stop and ask: "What is the nature of life? What is going on here? What or who is seeing?" You're better off asking astronomers and quantum physicists those questions because they're in awe of the universe while doctors often deny and refuse to accept what they can't explain.

One of the nine categories of evidence that Mark discusses is that of after-death contacts or ADCs. I wrote about these over twenty years ago in *Love, Medicine & Miracles* and have experienced numerous others since then. If these are difficult for you to imagine, just find out for yourself. Sit in a room with parents whose children have died and they'll tell you fascinating stories of their children coming back. They feel safe in these groups and will share stories they won't speak about in public.

In one case, a woman—whose son had been dead for five years—shared this story. "I was driving down the parkway, when my son appeared in the road in front of me and said: 'Mom, slow down!' So I slowed down. As I came around the curve there were about ten cars that had skidded on a sheet of ice and because of what my son said, I wasn't involved in the accident."

I've experienced a number of ADCs with patients who passed on. I would be out jogging, which puts me in a trance state, and I'd hear a voice say good-bye. I'd come home and tell my wife that so-and-so had just died and an hour later we'd get the call from the family telling us that. I think these are people you have to be close to. The close relationship creates a conscious energy in some way, making it easier for the communication to occur. If you study quantum physics, you become aware that after you separate subatomic particles they act as if they are still together even though they are separated by a great distance.

These events usually happen when I'm out biking or running in the morning, which is my meditation time, and I hear voices talking to me. It isn't always those who have died. The morning our son called to say my father was going to die, a voice very clearly said to me, "How did your parents meet?" And I said, "I don't know." And the voice said, "Then ask your mother when you get to the hospital." That changed the entire day because when I arrived at my dad's hospital room, my first words were not how sorry or sad I was but, "How did you and dad meet?"

My mother said she was sitting on the beach with some girls who had a terrible reputation. My father and some other boys tossed coins to see who would take the other girls out. My father lost and had to take my mother out. We all started laughing. That day became a beautiful day with my mother telling stories that had everyone—including my father—smiling and pink cheeked, instead of looking like he was going to die. I thought he was going to say, "Hold it, why leave? I'm going to hang around." But when his last grandchild arrived, he took a breath and left. It became a day free of pain and filled with beauty and awe. And you say, "Where did this crazy question come from?" But I've had it happen enough to banish doubt about the reality of spirit, intelligence, energy, love and consciousness existing separate from the human body.

I also appreciate Mark's discussion of input from enlightened religions. These esoteric viewpoints recognize a fuller, higher understanding of God. I don't see God as a man or woman sitting somewhere. To me, God is more like the product of the undifferentiated potential which is the source of everything, and out of which comes the Creator, the One. What is the Creator? Intelligence, Energy, Love and Consciousness. I think this is why the number ten is so important and prominent in our myths and lives. The one and the nothing gives rise to the one. The computer system relies on the 1 and the 0, not to mention the Ten Commandments, ten fingers and toes, and so on.

Recognizing this more accurate nature of God helps us remember why religions exist in the first place. They are meant to be a path to God, a reminder of our spiritual natures. Religions are not a reason to be killing and trampling over each other because, 'My God is better than your God or you've got the wrong God and don't really understand.' Jesus talked about the wide gate and the narrow gate. The path of love is the difficult one, that's what is preached by all the great sages and prophets who began the religions.

Mark has also included a section on accessing personal sources of wisdom. There are experiential ways to develop an inner knowing that needs no scientific proof. For me, regular silence and meditation assist inner peace—a greater appreciation of the rhythms, beauty, and vast potential of the Universe. The intuitive wisdom of poets and artists also convinces me. When that mother said her son talked to her five years after he died, I wondered why he was so lazy and not back in another body doing something meaningful. The musical "Carousel" and talking to Brian Weiss helped me see the truth about time.

In the show 'Carousel,' a man dies and an angel asks him if he wants to go back and watch his daughter graduate from high school. He says "My daughter's a baby!" and she was when he died but now she's in high school. The angel answers 'Oh, there's no time up here." When I heard that, I thought, "OK, if Rogers and Hammerstein understand this, then it must be the truth and I can accept it."

As Mark notes, really accepting both our mortality and our immortality radically changes our lives. Aging, life changes, and death are easier to handle when we know that our essence survives physical death. The most difficult experience, of course, is outliving our children. When counseling parents whose children have died, first I listen. Then I ask them the question that life is about: "How do you want to use your pain? How does charcoal become a diamond? Will you start a support group and help others or dwell on the past and endlessly question why?"

I remind them their child is whole again and free of pain. I encourage them to focus on, "What can we learn from this, how can we use this pain to birth ourselves more fully and help the world? How can we not drown in our own tears and let them extinguish our departed loved one's candle?" We all need to prepare ourselves for these events because the longer we live, the more likely it is that loved ones deaths will precede ours.

Mark tackles thorny theological questions about the ultimate nature of evil, hell, and other concepts. To me, evil is about not responding to the pain of others. We must use the energy of our pain to help heal and to display compassion for others who are sick or suffering. We are here to serve and the number of years we are here is not the limiting factor, our behavior is. Who is lord over our lives? Who do we serve? What convinced and educated me is the following personal experience.

Now, I'm a scientist; I was skeptical about the topic of past lives. I questioned the validity of past life regressions even though Brian Weiss was a good friend who, as a medical student, worked with me in the operating room at Yale. Then I spontaneously experienced a past life regression. What fascinated me was, it explained a lot of things about my life, very meaningful things our children have done, things I get very emotional about that made no sense until I understood what had gone on in the past.

And now I have no hesitancy sharing it with people because I've lived it and for me it's a very real thing. But before reading further, think for a moment about how you would respond if you were Abraham and your Lord asked you to sacrifice your child.

One day I was on the phone with a friend of mine, telling her about my busy schedule. She asked, "Why are you living this life?" meaning, 'Why don't you slow down' but when she said that, I had an immediate vision of myself with a sword in my hand striking people. I told her what I was seeing and said maybe that's why I became a surgeon—to help people with a knife. The vision disappeared and we were back into a practical conversation over the phone.

A couple of months later, on a cross country flight while staring out the window of the plane, I had another spontaneous vision. The best way I can describe it is that it's like a movie screen going up and you're sitting alone in a movie theater watching yourself perform. To summarize the story, I saw myself as a knight being asked by my lord to kill the neighbor's daughter because her father was trespassing on our soil. I didn't want to and he said if I didn't I would be killed. So out of fear, I decided to do it. One night I went into her room to kill her in her sleep so it wouldn't be painful for her and her dog began to growl. I raised my sword and killed the dog and then turned toward her bed. Awakened by the noise, she turned toward me. I saw my wife's face and killed who is in this life my wife, Bobbie.

I cried for hours on that plane; I just sobbed and sobbed. When I landed, I called my wife and cried some more. It was just so incredibly real. I realized why I had cried in the past about things our children have said, things that have been done that touched me in this lifetime. For example, one of our children came home from school with a large canvas on which was repetitively painted the word "words." But if you print out 'words, words, words,' with no space between the words as he did, they become 'swordswordswords.' I thought, "Why would a child do that? What sense is there?" I framed it and put it up on my wall because it said something to me.

Then I read the story "Wolfen" in which a knight came home from the wars. He didn't see anyone: his wife, his baby, or his dog. He ran upstairs into the nursery and saw blood everywhere, his blood-covered dog, and the overturned crib. He drew his sword and killed his dog assuming it had killed his son. Then he lifts the overturned crib and finds a dead wolf and his living baby. He realizes he has just killed his beloved dog that had saved his child's life. When I heard that story, I burst into tears again. I could read this story to children and they would say, "Why are you crying? It's only a story!"

Our home has always been filled with animals in need, a refuge for literally hundreds of animals wandering around the house and outside. It struck me that this relationship with so many animals could have come from the guilt of killing an animal and that I am still trying to make up for the past. When these kinds of things begin to happen and connect with my life, I become less of a doubter. I also now know why looking into my wife's face has always been such a moving experience for me.

Now, to understand the question about Abraham, you have to realize that when I returned with the head and asked my lord if he was happy, he said he was not. I had performed the act out of fear because I had no faith in him. Had I said, "Yes," he would have known I had faith that no harm would come to the young woman. He would then have trusted me and asked me to return with her and her parents and see that we marry and create one family with nothing to fight over. So Abraham's and Isaac's faith in their Lord allowed them to say, 'Yes,' knowing the ultimate result would not be a destructive one.

The bottom line? Even if you conclude that this is all total nonsense, if it helps you live your life in a healthier, happier way—then it's meaningful. If we see life as a school, then you've just moved up a grade and have increased your wisdom. You'll be more likely to help others and be more understanding and that's really what it's all about.

The diverse collection of evidence in *Soul Proof* helps us remember that death is not an end, but a transition and a new beginning. We can then more clearly focus on the truth that we came here not to be served but to serve for the good of the many. Let us know deeply that we are born again and again on the wheel of rebirth so that again and again we may offer our bodies, minds, and spirits for the benefit of others.

Remember what God told me, "Graduations are not called terminations but commencements. The *Bible* ends in *Revelations*, not conclusions and life is no different. It is a series of beginnings. I can tell you the only thing of permanence is love so if you seek immortality, love someone. As an outside advisor to the board of directors of heaven, I know what I am talking about.

Bernie Siegel, M.D.
—author of *Love, Medicine and Miracles;*
Prescriptions For Living, and other books

Soul
PROOF

Compelling evidence we are immortal
spiritual beings—and what that means for our lives!

Introduction

"Let us live as if we were immortal." - Aristotle

When I was nineteen-years-old, I worked part-time as a respiratory therapist. On one of my first calls to the emergency room, we worked on a five-year-old boy who had been hit by a truck. As we treated him, the story unfolded: he had been walking to his first day of kindergarten and was the only child of young parents. Despite hours of resuscitative care, he died from multiple injuries. In shock, I stumbled out into the hall just in time to see his parents' faces contort in grief as a doctor told them the news.

I went outside, shook my fist at the sky, and cursed God. How could an all loving, powerful, and knowing God allow a little one to die so tragically? What kind of world was this where innocent children suffer and die and people experience such losses? Afterwards, I entered a period of agnosticism and experienced the emotional pain and confusion that accompany a bleak spiritual perspective.

Over time, this and other difficult events in my life motivated me to search for answers to life's existential questions such as: 'Who am I? Why am I here? Is there a loving, just God? Why is there so much suffering? What happens after I die?' You know the questions. I began a quest to prove to myself whether or not God and the afterlife really exist.

After thirty years of intense searching, I've assembled convincing proof that we each really are timeless spiritual beings who are here to learn, love, serve and enjoy. There is a Divine Presence whose love and fairness know no bounds. We suffer when we forget to view life from a spiritual perspective. For example, that little boy's "tragedy" compelled me to find sensible answers to life's most difficult questions. Since then, thousands of people have been helped by my outreaches and I'm just getting warmed up. So was his death a tragedy or a victory?

Now I invite you to consider two important and powerfully life-changing questions.

First, what would it take for you to be convinced that you really are a timeless spiritual being who eternally experiences life both before and after physical death? Are you like a Miami talk-show host who told me he would only believe in afterlife when he saw an embalmed corpse climb out of a casket? If so, you will have to wait until you pass over and see for yourself.

But maybe you are more open-minded than our radio host friend. What if you knew that many people—including renowned scientists, famous individuals, and probably some of your loved ones—have had *firsthand experiences* of spirit beings? Would it help to know that denominations in *every religion and spiritual wisdom source* believe in universal salvation, an eventual heavenly afterlife *for all*? Would you be more convinced if you knew that ground-breaking *clinical and scientific research* strongly indicates a continuity of consciousness?

My second question is: if—as the evidence suggests—we all really are immortal souls, how would that change your life? Would it help to know that you *can't ever lose* loved ones, but are only separated for awhile? Could you better survive, and even thrive, through life's changes if you deeply grasped that you are eternal by nature, an indestructible being of energy? Might this knowledge assist your life in many ways and improve the way you treat yourself and others?

Take a few moments and think about these questions. As I present the highlights of this evidence, please feel as though we are having a one-on-one discussion about these important issues. Internalizing the evidence in this book allows a growing realization of just how exciting, fair, and safe our earthly sojourns are. You can connect with the tangible—and sometimes instantaneous— benefits that accompany a deeper apprehension of our undying natures.

My wish is that you will enjoy the many great benefits of an internalized knowing about your true soul nature. These include:

1. Experiencing little or no fear and grief about your own "death and dying" and that of your loved ones

2. Greater trust about all the rhythms of life, even those involving suffering and tragedy

3. A deeper understanding, or least peace, about life's existential questions: Who am I, why am I here, Is there a God, what happens when we die, and so on?

4. Increased clarity and courage to follow your purpose and heartfelt joys

5. More peace and acceptance about aging and bodily degeneration

6. Feeling closer to and grateful for God and the heavenly host

7. Appreciation for and optimal care of your soul's bodily temple

8. Resolute knowledge that living—and dying—are totally safe, fair, and purposeful

9. Excitement about a joyful eternity of loving, learning, enjoying, and serving

I'll discuss one of these benefits briefly after each category of evidence.

Even a *glimpse* of spiritual enlightenment can radically improve your life, especially during tough times. As "Martha" from England wrote after reading excerpts of *Soul Proof*: ""I have read your newsletters for about three months now and I want to say 'thank you' because I have learned so much from them. My son and dad died two years ago and your information has been a great comfort during my grieving. Keep up the fabulous articles; you are helping many people understand what life and the afterlife are all about."

Earth is a difficult place to live, I know. Like most of us, I've grieved over loved ones who have passed on. Broken relationships have saddened and haunted me. I've experienced cruelty, disappointments, unfulfilled dreams, financial loss, depression, and health challenges. Despite the beauty and many positive attributes of planet earth, life here is no picnic. Hardships, loss, and eventual death are integral parts of the human experience.

No one is immune from these struggles and every age group experiences different trials and tribulations. Two teenagers recently wrote me after reading pre-publication copies of *Soul Proof*. "Tom" a 16 year old from the U.S. said, "Your book changed my life spiritually. I now feel happier about myself. You helped me put what my subconscious was 'feeling' into conscious 'thinking'. I really am an eternal soul; thanks to you, I now realize this. This may sound like a small thing, but—to me—it is just the beginning." "Susan" a 14 year old from South Africa wrote, "You've definitely improved my outlook on life. I now feel that I can make the most of it, fulfill my potential here on earth, and look forward to the afterlife. Thanks again!"

These young people have beautifully described the powerful implications that stem from the evidence presented in this book. The bottom line? No matter what does or doesn't happen to you, it's OK, it's safe, you'll survive it. To paraphrase Nietzsche, that which does not kill you makes you stronger—and *nothing* can kill your spirit. Your real self is much more resilient and mighty than any difficulties you might encounter.

Look at it this way. Do you worry and grieve the next day after watching a movie in which the main character struggles or dies? Of course not—it's just a movie. Well, in your life's movie, you—as a soul—are the producer, director and actor. Much collective evidence strongly indicates that our relatively brief lives on earth are very much like movies. Life is like a play, a drama, a learning experience. Our true selves have lived before and will live after this and every episode.

Let me assure you that I am eminently qualified to write and teach about this subject. My credentials include graduate training in theology, clinical psychology, and chiropractic health care. While working in hospitals, I was present with hundreds of people at the time of death. Other clinical experiences in my thirty year career include providing psychological counseling and private practice as a holistically oriented physician.

I have been a guest on many radio and TV shows discussing soul and after-life topics and have lectured extensively across the country. In addition, I hosted a nationally syndicated radio show and interviewed top experts in these fields like Drs. Brian Weiss, Bernie Siegel, Wayne Dyer, Ken Ring, Michael Newton and others. I have also personally used yoga, meditation, breath work, optimal lifestyle habits, and other transformative techniques for many years.

These credentials and experiences are important, but here's what really makes me passionate about this work. I've personally had out-of-body experiences, multi-sensory apprehensions of spirit beings and Spirit, and clairaudient perceptions. Over the years, I've also repeatedly seen the transcendence that occurs when people realize their lives are not going to end or result in a fiery eternity. In my own life and in the lives of all those I've been privileged to teach and touch, I've observed a new, powerful awareness emerging. The realization that we each really are timeless spiritual beings empowers us to dramatically change our lives, beliefs, and energies for the better.

Faith and Knowledge

The fear of death is paramount, so much so that it haunts most people and causes problems in nearly everyone's lives. Many people are uncomfortable being with dying persons, going to funerals, and knowing what to say to mourners. Inordinate amounts of grief are suffered because of the erroneous notions that death is an end, that a heavenly reward is for only a select few, or that loved ones may be in hell for eternity.

Death anxiety also negatively impacts upon society via bizarre behaviors stemming from the denial of death. Unconscious attempts at escaping the "Grim Reaper" can include excessive attention to physical appearance, blatant materialism, frequent or dysfunctional relationships, and self-destructive behaviors such as eating disorders or drug and alcohol abuse.

We each need a strong, rational basis for our belief systems about the afterlife. In the past, traditional religions attempted to provide this, but most people are no longer convinced by faith alone. Many have rejected orthodoxy; in fact, only a minority of U.S. households now regularly attends worship services. People would like to believe that we are immortal denizens of an equitable universe if only they could see more objective and empirical evidence.

This book provides that evidence. It need not detract from your religious or spiritual beliefs; in fact, this proof further validates most teachings. The information in *Soul Proof* allows you to enjoy a strong personal faith and objective knowledge about your soul nature. This combination will powerfully enable you to live with courage and hope—not fear and despair. Having a broad based knowledge and a faith-filled perspective is the best foundation for joyous, empowered and successful living now and for evermore.

Categories of Evidence

Nine categories of fascinating and wide-ranging evidence strongly indicate that our real selves do not die. Reading *Soul Proof* is like having *Cliff Notes* for the class "Afterlife 101." I've researched hundreds of books, attended many seminars, and traveled widely to compile all the available evidence. My own firsthand experiences and those of many clients over the years are also discussed. I summarized all of this complex information for you in a simple, interesting, and easy-to-read format.

There are many scientific, clinical, religious, and firsthand indications of *immortality for all*. I especially emphasize *validation cases* that have been confirmed and are difficult or impossible to explain otherwise. Taken altogether, this evidence strongly points to the reality of our timeless soul natures and, hence, afterlife for all.

The nine categories of evidence include:

1. after-death contact cases
2. near-death and out-of-body experiences
3. miraculous events and divine revelations
4. scientific input
5. paranormal indications
6. religious and spirituality teachings
7. peri-natal input
8. reincarnation evidence
9. firsthand experience and inner knowing

By the way, if any of the categories seem too strange to you, don't read them. Please don't deny yourself the many benefits of this information because your religious or personal beliefs aren't completely compatible with all the evidence.

Even Evelyn, the woman whose quote is on the back cover said, "I don't know about that reincarnation stuff but . . ." and then continued her endorsement.

Keep in mind that only *one* event in *one* category need be true for the thesis of afterlife to be adequately proven. As noted philosopher and physician William James said, "In order to disprove the law that all crows are black, it is enough to find one white crow." As you will see, there is no reasonable explanation for all this evidence unless, in fact, consciousness indeed exists independent of the human experience.

Woven throughout these nine categories are three basic *ways of knowing* that a greater spiritual reality exists and we each are integral parts of it. The first is through accepting and incorporating *enlightened religious and spiritual teachings*. Traditionally, many people have relied solely on doctrines of their own religion and respective holy books. This is an excellent start but lacks the other verifiable and experiential components that can complement ones faith.

Secondly, a growing body of scientific and clinical evidence further points to a continuity of consciousness for all. Included is verifiable research on near-death experiences, after-death contacts, out-of-body experiences, past-life events, peri-natal awareness, and data from authentic mediums. Advanced physics and chemistry also explain the indestructibility of energy, the illusion of physical solidity, and the relative reality of time, space and matter.

A third way of knowing is empirical, that is, gained through direct *personal experience*. This is the most impressive type of proof for those fortunate enough to have mystical, revelatory, or paranormal experiences. Valid firsthand experiences are beyond the need of proof for those who have them. The resulting *inner knowing* is ultimately indescribable and radically strengthens ones spiritual faith.

Communicating the Unspeakable

Regarding speaking about ultimate truths, ancient Eastern wisdom states, 'He who knows does not speak and he who speaks does not know.' This sentence addresses the relatively unknowable nature of God, afterlife, and otherworldly subjects. Despite an abundance of knowledge about afterlife and soul issues, there is still much we do not know. This is the "X factor", the Divine Mystery that makes definitive statements difficult or impossible. Perhaps this is as it should be. Maybe we need to leave room for Spirit to breathe and move, to honor a sacred space for the expansion and change that is Life unfolding.

Having said that, there is much that we can now—in the 21st century—state with certainty. I am sensitive to the semantics of scientific methodology and the importance of not overstating the evidence. At the same time, I want readers to understand that there is much information that strongly points to ever unfolding spiritual realities for all people. At times, I will mention what makes the most sense to me, but my beliefs and understandings have been mightily shaped by this cumulative evidence.

Webster defines *evidence* as: "an outward sign; something that furnishes proof; testimony." The definition of *proof* is: "something proved by common experience; knowledge acquired by experience; something that induces certainty and establishes validity." (1) Based on these definitions, this book presents *both evidence and proof* that we each really are souls. However, since the word "proof" also has connotations of double-blind and replicated research in peer-reviewed published journals, I sometimes use other terms such as 'appears, indicates, suggests, points to' and so on.

Establishing a commonly agreed upon vocabulary is vital for clearly discussing nonphysical dimensions. Please remember that any terms indicating separateness are based on a model of dualism, that is, the theory that mutually irreducible differences comprise reality. Examples of dualism are Creator and creation, mind and matter, or spirit and physicality. These supposed divisions may appear to exist from our limited human perspectives. While language that supports duality might seem to simplify communication, it actually confounds a more accurate realization of unitive consciousness. From all the available data, it appears that the most accurate understanding of reality is that *all life is inseparably One.*

That all life is connected means that our real selves, our spiritual aspects, are of primary importance. The physical, while relatively important, is very transitory by comparison and merely houses our souls for a brief time. Some data suggests that only part of the soul's energy is involved in this earthly sojourn; the other part never leaves spiritual dimensions. In this sense, our souls never fully leave the Light.

The purest understandings of absolute truth, then, recognize that there is no separation among creation. Any perceived division is an *illusion* or, at best, only a relatively real perception of reality. But many people can't fully fathom this model yet—it's too abstract. As such, discussions using a dualistic model serve as stepping stones for apprehending the truth of oneness more clearly. And so I will speak of God, angels, spirit guides, and humans as if these are really separate entities.

The term 'God' has been greatly misused and misunderstood over time. To many, the word still denotes a large, white-bearded man that judges, smites, and condemns while sitting on a throne way up in the sky. As such, I often use other synonyms that include: the Light, Source, Great Spirit, Presence, Ground of All Being, Infinite, Divine, Universal Intelligence, Spirit, and Oneness. The term Mother/Father God recognizes that this level of energy is beyond gender; as such, I alternatively refer to the Creator as He, She, or It. All of these terms are capitalized to denote absolute levels of wisdom, love, and peace.

Most importantly, remember that, as Buckminster Fuller said, the universe is friendly. So please keep in mind that when speaking of God—no matter what the term—I am *not* referring to a huge guy in the sky with a bad attitude, but, rather, the ultimate source and well-spring of energy, power, and consciousness. The Sanskrit root word 'ananda'—meaning supreme existence, knowledge, bliss—captures the nature of this Presence quite well.

The *heavenly host* or *spiritual support team* are names I use for God's celestial assistants: ascended masters, angels, and advanced spirit guides. These facets of Spirit are much more aware of their interconnectedness with the Ground of All Being. From a duality model, they are higher and purer manifestations of energy with faster vibratory rates than humans.

Terms used for realms where greater spiritual awareness reigns more consistently than on earth include: heaven, other side, spirit world, spiritual dimension, and spirit side. The synonym 'Home' is capitalized to differentiate that realm from our temporary earthly homes. Quotation marks are used with the word 'hell' because of its relatively transient and illusory nature.

Terms for entities living in spiritual darkness include: unenlightened souls, malicious or capricious spirits, or unawakened souls. Evidence indicates that these unfortunate souls have no real power in the presence of Divine Love and Light. Souls that haven't yet embraced the Presence suffer in various degrees of temporary "hells", but this is not an irreversible predicament. A personified evil being—"satan or the devil"—is considered to be real by some. Evidence suggests, however, that there is no formidable negative power opposed to God. Any seeming temporary darkness reveals its illusory nature when exposed to the Light.

More accurate terms for the misnomers 'death and dying' include: pass over, change worlds, cross over, pass on, leave the body, graduate, transition, and drop the body. The term 'deceased' is also useful as it implies a departure from physical life. These descriptors indicate that passing on is a next step, a promotion, a flight to potentially higher ground. The words 'die' or 'death' are emotionally laden and convey an end or loss. As such, they will sometimes be used with quotation marks to highlight the vast evidence that no one really dies. If only the earthly body ceases to exist, the terms 'physical death' and 'bodily death' are also more accurate descriptors.

Some people refer to their current age as "body age" to remind themselves and others that our souls are timeless and it's just the body that ages. Others refer to the body as an "earth suit" to remember that the body merely houses the infinite spirit for a while.

Soul mates or *cluster mates* are those spiritual entities with whom we have had different relationships throughout time and space. Reports from the other side say we each have many such kindred spirits from our on-going groups in nonphysical realms. *Primary* soul mates are very close while *secondary* ones are less so.

Finally, terms used for the *soul*, that extension of the Source in each of us, include: real self, consciousness, awareness, true self, inner self, spiritual self, innate intelligence, enduring self, eternal self, mind, inner being, and infinite self. The word *spirit* is also used but differs from the capitalized form, Spirit, which is a synonym for God.

Final Comments

The benefits of this book are quite practical and can be applied to every aspect of your life from this moment on. Life makes much more sense and flows better when you really know who you are. This freedom from fear was beautifully described by "Jill" from New Zealand who wrote, "I ordered your book a few months ago and was pleased, delighted, and fascinated with the information within. A few weeks ago I was diagnosed with cancer. Interestingly, while the doctor gave the prognosis to me, I found myself calm and surrounded by what I can only describe as love. I honestly feel that reading your book helped marshal my courage and faith to deal with this crisis."

Discovering the 'good news that sets us free' has certainly made a huge difference in my life and it can in yours as well. Although I present this evidence as objectively as possible, it is impracticable for me to hide my personal convictions. My deeply held beliefs led me to write this book and shaped the way I discuss each category. Based on my research and many life experiences, I am convinced that dying is totally safe. Yes, our outer shells change and eventually drop away, but we each are much more than our bodies.

There is no doubt in my mind about it: we are timeless souls, eternal spirit beings, continuous manifestations of energy. This immortal aspect of ourselves is part and parcel of God and is indestructible. Our real selves can't and don't "die." Many cultures celebrate the transition from formed to formless dimensions and rightly so. Those who pass on have graduated from this physical experience. Their souls evidently fulfilled required lessons and moved on to the next set of growth opportunities.

I know with every fiber of my being that a heavenly eternal life is always an open-ended possibility for each one of us, no strings attached. Creator *is* love, life, and eternal energy and so is Her creation. We each have the potential to reflect our high natures, to be bright and veritable torches of light. My strong, internalized knowing carries me through life's tough times. "Death" and aging are just transitory stages in life—just as important and necessary as birth and youth.

My inner assurance that we *all* can enjoy a sublime life after death makes it easier for me to accept life's changes. "Losing" loved ones, whether they pass on or when relationships change, is easier because I know that I can see them again and love is one of the few constants in life. Observing my body starting to age has also been less scary given my knowledge that life is forever, albeit ever changing. I'm not too thrilled about aging and all that goes with it, but that's part of life. Life's changes can feel like losses until I remember they are fleeting mileposts as I journey through eternity.

I am personally certain about all of these things, but I can't believe for you. Only you can decide for yourself what seems most true. The information in *Soul Proof* will help you make wise conclusions based on all the available indicators. I encourage you to examine this evidence with an open-minded and critical analysis then decide for yourself what makes sense. My hope is that these additional pieces of the puzzle will help you make more sense of this challenging yet supremely special and beautiful world.

One of the working titles for this book was *Coming Home.* No matter what our circumstances in life, when we *remember*—who we are, where we came from, and Who walks beside us—we are always Home.

This wisdom is reflected in the wonderful book *Go Toward The Light* by Chris Oyler. When her son Ben, a nine-year-old dying from AIDS, asked about the nature of heaven, his dad replied: "We don't know exactly what it looks like. But it will feel like coming home. You know what it's like to get back home after you've been away for awhile? You know how good it feels? That's what it will be like—like going home." (2)

That's how we increasingly feel as we become spiritually enlightened.

My greatest wish is that this evidence will help you live with more courage, wisdom, joy, and peace. I pray that this information will help you really know that your true self is unique, important, powerful, and imperishable. There's no one else quite like you; humanity needs the contributions of all available realized beings. May you always deeply know and vibrantly reflect your high soul nature.

By the way, the title *Soul Proof* has a double meaning:

1. Much proof exists that we are souls

2. As such, we each are "soul proof", just as a watch is "shock proof" or "water proof." That is, our enduring selves—our souls—do not die and cannot be hurt by anything.

After-death Contacts

'An old man is lying alone in his bed on a cold wintry night. He is miserly, cruel and selfish—and sees nothing wrong with all of that. He hears a noise and looks over to see three ghosts who take him on an odyssey that radically transforms his life for the better.' You may recognize this character as Scrooge in Charles Dickens' *A Christmas Carol*. The inspiration for this story may have come from real life experience.

In his writings, Dickens described walking alone late at night along a darkened cobblestone street. Suddenly, he heard the sound of hoof beats and looked over his shoulder to see a horse and its rider careening rapidly toward him. He lunged into a doorway to avoid being run over and, then—to his surprise—saw nothing. The street was suddenly as quiet and unoccupied as it had been a moment before. (1)

This experience and perhaps others convinced him about the reality of spirits and may have influenced him to write about Scrooge's spirit-assisted rebirth. *A Christmas Carol* has entertained and inspired many people over the years and serves as a potent metaphor for the transformative potential of visitation by spirits.

Dickens wasn't alone. After-death contacts—ADCs—have been reported across recorded time and in many cultures. Famous people like President Abraham Lincoln and Sir Arthur Conan Doyle had personal experiences that convinced them of the reality of the spirit world. General George Patton strongly believed in ghosts and claims to have received visits by departed loved ones such as his father. As he told his nephew, Fred Ayer, Jr., who wrote Patton's memoirs *Before the Colors Fade*: "Father used to come to me in the evenings in my tent and sit down to talk and assure me that I would do all right and act bravely in the battle coming the next day. He was just as real as in his study at home at Lake Vineyard." (2)

The phenomenon of after-death contacts is a fascinating category of evidence that humans survive bodily death. The term ADC describes contact with a "deceased" person who is in a nonphysical dimension. Such reports used to be considered weird and most people did not share them for fear of being considered crazy. Now more people are openly sharing these surprisingly common experiences. After-death contacts have been reported by 25% of Americans, 66% of widows, and 75% of parents whose children have passed over.

I was reminded about the commonality of ADCs recently as I prepared for a TV interview on the subject and spoke with the producer. She excitedly said, "Oh, I've had some of those!" and shared several including the following: "When I was about three years old, I awoke one morning at my grandmother's house and went into the kitchen. I saw a soldier standing there. He looked like a real person to me but I didn't know him so I didn't ask him to make my breakfast or help me get dressed. When my grandmother came downstairs to help me, I told her about the man in the kitchen and asked who he was. She became very upset and wouldn't talk about it any further. Only years later did I figure out who this man was when I found an old picture of him. It was my grandfather; he had been a soldier and my grandmother was widowed when my mother was an infant."

As you will learn, respected views from science and religion support the possibility of communication from beyond the grave. For example, Rev. Dr. Norman Vincent Peale, who earned worldwide respect for his sensible and practical application of religious principles, stated, "I firmly believe that when you die you will enter immediately into another life. They who have gone before us are alive in one form of life and we in another." (3)

Some religious denominations believe that the deceased sleep for a long, long time until a universal resurrection and judgment day. However, much collective evidence is consistent with Peale's view that life continues on seamlessly after death. A number of other religions and denominations also describe an uninterrupted continuation of consciousness. As such, ADC reports are consistent with at least some well-accepted theological constructs.

I first became aware of ADCs when I worked in hospitals as a respiratory therapist. Several older but completely lucid patients reservedly told me, "I don't know why I'm telling you this but there's something about you. Last night I was visited by my late husband. He stood right there by the foot of the bed, smiled, and told me I would see him again." Each time, these patients passed on within forty-eight hours. Reports of this type involved a visit by their departed spouse or parent. These patients were totally coherent and very excited about their experience but hesitant to tell others for fear of being thought they were crazy.

ADCs often occur during dreams, probably because the receiving party is deeply relaxed and the usual brain activity is dampened. These dreams often are more vibrant and realistic than usual and the dreamer awakens with a strong sense that actual contact was made with a departed loved one. Some contain evidence that suggest it was more than just a dream. The eminent psychiatrist Carl Jung related a personal dream ADC: "Six weeks after his death my father appeared to me in a dream. . . It was an unforgettable experience, and it forced me for the first time to think about life after death." (4)

What is the difference between ghosts and these souls who visit loved ones during ADCs? Ghosts are in limbo between earth and spirit world as a result of several possibilities. These include: intense addictions; strong emotions such as revenge and anger; a sudden or violent death; and limited spiritual knowledge with resistance to entering the Light. Being stuck in this netherworld parallels purgatory or minor "hells" described by some religions. Ghosts can enter the Light anytime they choose, but may be afraid or ignorant about this possibility. Visitations by these forlorn spirits may seem scary or sad. Their energy is slow, darker, and feels hopeless.

Souls who visit during ADCs, on the other hand, usually make brief visits and exude energies of peace and light. They are not stuck, but, rather, have successfully made the transition into spirit world and are "just visiting" our physical dimension. Their visits are voluntary and are motivated by love and the desire to relay comfort and hope. Such encounters are considered sacred and they often transform the recipients forever.

I've been asked about the importance of letting loved ones go and not grieving so excessively so that they are hesitant to leave the earth plane. This is wise counsel since newly departed souls might delay their entry into the Light because of extreme mourning and attachment by loved ones. This delay is by choice, however, and they are not stuck. They can go into the Light after attempting to comfort the bereaved. Later, after they're settled in their celestial abode, they can visit via ADCs.

Why do some departed souls make contact and others don't? They may be busy with other demands, may have reincarnated already, or may not be able to energetically make the contact. Reports from spirit side say that much energy and determination are required for a spirit-being to make significant contact in physical dimensions. The receptivity of those on earth is also a very important factor since being calm and open-minded improves receptive abilities.

∞ ∞ ∞ ∞ ∞

I've divided ADCs into four subcategories: shared, evidential, transformational and facilitated.

Shared ADCs

"Shared ADCs" is a term for those after-death contacts experienced by more than one person at the same time. Most after-death contacts occur with only one person at a time and, while they may be personally convincing, they often lack any verifiable aspects. By being perceived by more than one person simultaneously, shared ADCs provide an additional validation component. This enhanced authenticity strongly indicates that the contact is not wishful thinking or an over-active imagination, but, rather, an objective contact with departed loved ones.

My daughters' piano teacher, Nancy Arthur, shared the following shared ADC:

> My mother departed this life in 1999 at age 94. She had been a schoolteacher and a very intellectual woman who read voraciously. She and I had explored the paranormal and read much on reincarnation. It seemed rational to her as it did to me.
>
> At her death, my two siblings and I inherited several pieces of long-time family real estate. My husband, daughters, and I were gathered around my computer as my sister from Louisiana

emailed the estate appraisal to us—low, of course, for tax purposes. Mother's small house in town, the two farms, and her heirloom antiques were of great sentimental value to her and we hoped that she wasn't offended by the low estimate.

Suddenly, the phone beside the computer began to ring. We were dumb-founded since it was the only one out of several in the house that was ringing and it definitely WAS NOT PLUGGED IN! I picked up the receiver to stop the ringing and said, "Mother?" in a quivery voice but there was no answer. I guess mom was displeased at those paltry estimates of her earthly treasures.

One of my newsletter subscribers, Cynthia Bellini Olsen in Colorado, sent me this incredible ADC story that was shared by numerous family members:

Early this year, my precious sister Pat made her transition from the physical world. The previous fall, my partner Robert and I had stayed at her place for two months. During that time we discovered her closets were filled with mothballs. When we asked why, she said a friend had reorganized her closets and put them there. The smell was intolerable to Robert and me but didn't seem to bother Pat in the least. We threw them out.

Within a week after Pat died *at my brother's house,* mothballs unexplainably appeared in various places there: under beds, on the kitchen floor, in the living room where she had been—all areas that had been frequently swept. My brother and sister-in-law, Bob and Sharon, found six more under a couch that had been moved after Pat died. They later found more mothballs in the room where she had passed.

Finally, Sharon asked Pat to 'please stop with the moth balls' as her asthma was really affected by that odor. I asked Pat if she could choose another scent to scatter around. A few days later, Bob and Sharon were sitting in the living room and the scent of roses filled the air. It was so strong and there were absolutely no fresh flowers in the house or yard at that time.

Upon our return to Colorado, Robert and I discovered three more mothballs in the bag that contained Pat's ashes. On two other occasions, several of us found three more on the lawn near our front door. These unexplainable incidences continue to mystify us. Pat had tremendous will power and determination throughout her life and it apparently has persisted on the other side. What a clever way to grab our attention and contact us. Her spiritual essence, even in the form of mothballs, will always be with us until we are reunited once again.

A long-time patient of mine, Ted, passed over after suffering with lung cancer. His wife Elizabeth is a salt-of-the-earth Christian woman whom I have known for many years and trust completely. She told me about a unique shared ADC that happened after she prayed for a sign that Ted was at peace. In the first spring after Ted's burial, the family planted flowers by his grave and videotaped the scenery. As soon as they arrived at the grave site, a sparrow flew to Ted's monument and perched there, cocking its head and looking intently at the family.

Elizabeth remarked that it seemed as though the sparrow was trying to tell them something or that perhaps Ted's soul was communicating through the bird. Throughout their visit, the same sparrow continued to chirp and hop on the grave stone. The family excitedly videotaped the bird with the idea of showing it to other family members. When they played the tape at home, however, there was the grave site, grass, trees, family members, and flowers—but no sparrow! They considered this anomaly to be a sign from Ted. This story also corroborates reports that spirit beings are difficult to capture on film.

Sharon, a friend whose word I trust implicitly, contributed this shared ADC: "There was a man who lived up the hill from us when I was young. He liked to work in his yard and was always planting something or trimming the grass. One day, he became ill and had to go to the hospital. The following day, my mother and I were outside and saw him getting some tools out of his shed. She said our neighbor must be better because he was out of the hospital and preparing to do some yard work. But later that day we got the newspaper and saw that he had died at the hospital the day before."

Evidential ADCs

The next category of validation ADCs is termed *evidential* and includes experiences in which a person learns something he or she did not know before and, in fact, had no way of knowing. Information revealed by evidential ADCs provides stronger documentation that these encounters are not illusions. Visiting spirits may tell about long lost objects which are subsequently discovered. Even more impressively, they may relay information that was not known to anyone but is later verified.

An example of this type is provided by Bill and Judy Guggenheim in *Hello from Heaven*. As Kitty, a sixty-five year-old homemaker in Alabama described:

Leland was our friend, and we bought our home from him. He was a mail carrier and was killed one morning in his mail truck.

The next morning he appeared in my bedroom! While standing there, he told me to tell Frances, his wife, that he had an insurance policy she didn't know about. He said, "It's in our bedroom, in the top drawer of the chest under the paper. Tell Frances where it is." And then he disappeared.

My husband, Cliff, walked in the room and I told him what had happened. He said, "Well, let's call and tell Frances." I said, "She'll think I'm nuts!"

So my husband went down and told Leland's brother, Reed, to look in the top drawer of the chest under the paper—that he might find an insurance policy there. But Cliff didn't explain what had happened to me.

Sure enough, they looked and there was an insurance policy just like Leland had told me! Reed called and thanked my husband, but we never told them how we knew. They just wouldn't have understood. (5)

I recently attended a high school graduation party for the daughter of close friends and heard the following ADC that has both shared and evidential aspects. While talking with the family, I shared a bit about my upcoming book and the various categories of evidence. When I mentioned after-death contacts, one of the grandmothers interrupted me and said, "I had one of those!"

She turned to her daughter and said, "Remember when Helen was so ill and close to dying? Ruthie and I were on the front porch and we saw the same thing at the same time: a white ghostly shape appeared out of nowhere in the yard in front of us, moved across the yard, and then suddenly disappeared. I turned to Ruthie and said what we both knew: 'Helen must have just passed on.'" She continued, "We went into the house and she had just died. When you see something like that—and someone else does too—you know without a doubt that death isn't the end!"

In *Love, Medicine, and Miracles*, Bernie Siegel, M.D., shares an evidential case involving Bill, a physician with esophageal cancer. He had joined an Exceptional Cancer Patient group but was quiet and distant. Says Siegel:

> Three months after Bill had died of his cancer, a young college student came to my office to interview me. She said she'd been in a healing circle the night before, and since they knew she was going to see me the next day, the medium who was directing the circle had asked if there was any message for me. She handed me a card: "To Bernie from Bill with love and peace. If I had known it was this easy, I'd have bought the package a long time ago and wouldn't have resisted so much."

> When I called his wife, she said, "That's what he always told me after the meetings. He would attend, but he said he couldn't buy the package." . . . The people in the healing circle knew nothing about who Bill was, yet there was the same phrase he and his wife used. "Love and peace" is the closing I use for all my letters. Who else could this note be from? How can I help but believe and share this belief with others? (6)

Elisabeth Kubler-Ross, M.D., had an evidentiary encounter with a deceased patient. She was walking in the hallway toward her office one day and noticed a woman standing in the corridor. They began talking and Dr. Kubler-Ross led the woman into her office. After a while, she said with considerable amazement 'I know you!' and recognized the woman as 'Mrs. Schwartz,' a patient who had died several months earlier. Mrs. Schwartz acknowledged her identity and the two talked for some period of time. In an attempt to obtain verifiable evidence of the visit, Dr. Kubler-Ross asked the woman to write a note to her minister. Afterwards, analysis of the handwriting matched samples written before she passed over. (7)

Parenthetically, Dr. Kubler-Ross most likely didn't initially recognize the woman because apparitions of the deceased typically appear younger than they did before crossing over. When taking on a physical appearance, souls who were older when they passed on usually appear to be about thirty-five years old.

Transformational ADCs

Transformational ADCs, although not confirmatory in nature, are proof enough for the person involved. These are usually experienced by only one person so there is no shared or validation component to it. Nonetheless, those who experience such ADCs are changed radically and their stories often ring true to listeners. I've received many of these reports from those whose lives I touch via my books, newsletters, and workshops.

Dorothy, a spry and wise octogenarian, wrote that her first ADC happened many years ago: "My grandmother had died several years before I went to work in Washington D.C.; we had been very close before her death. It was January 14, 1944, and that evening, as I was preparing for bed, my closet door opened slightly, and I felt a tangible presence. An audible, gentle voice said, 'I'm so proud of you that you left home and are working here and I know that you will do well.' My memory is still so clear about that moment. The next day I called my mother in Ohio; she said they had put flowers on the altar at church for Grandma, as it was her birthday. I told her about my 'visitation' and she cried."

During one of my radio interviews, an elderly widower from Florida called in to share the following story. He had bought his wife a music box for a wedding anniversary but it had quit working many years ago. Shortly after she passed on, she made her spiritual presence known, he felt, when the box started playing. He had not wound the spring and it still sat on the shelf where it had all those years. Yet, periodically throughout the year—especially on birthdays and anniversaries—the music box played perfectly. He was convinced that her soul was contacting him from another realm, reminding him that they would see each other again.

Over the years, I have heard several ADC reports involving music boxes; perhaps those in spirit world are as enchanted as we by those simple melodies. My good friend Nancy had a music box that had been broken for many years. Just before she received news of her mother-in-law's passing, the box started playing. A couple days later, while Nancy was reading the obituary, it tinkled again. She says, "I still get goose bumps when I remember this happening."

During another radio interview, the host told a high-tech ADC story. A husband and wife had a secret code on their pagers that no one else knew. When one of them was to call home, the other dialed in 777-7777. The wife passed on and soon after her burial, the husband visited the cemetery. As he approached her gravesite, his pager beeped. He was astounded and grateful as he saw on the display: 777-7777.

Departed pets can also visit from spirit side as illustrated by the following powerful transformational ADC story that blessed several people over time. Heidi from Pennsylvania had a cat named Lucky that passed over at age twenty-one. She states:

I wasn't a religious person and never really believed in life after death but the following experience in 1990 changed my beliefs. I had just laid down in bed for the night. I was still awake when I felt that someone was calling for me. I sat up and thought, "I can't go. If Bill (her husband) wakes up he'll wonder where I am." That didn't seem to matter because before I knew it I was going down our hall. I didn't make the conscious decision to go and I actually do not remember getting up and walking.

I noticed a very bright light coming from our son's bedroom. I looked in and saw my cat Lucky who had passed on about 4 months earlier. She was rolling around on her back the way cats do when they feel good. She appeared young and didn't have her arthritis anymore. I was amazed at how bright it was in the room. I looked at the window and thought, "the sun isn't out and the light in the room isn't this bright."

I knew that someone was behind me. It seemed like the person was dressed in a white robe; I felt it was Jesus. I remember thinking how warm and peaceful I felt—I had never felt anything like it. I looked down at my feet but it was like they weren't there. I reached for my cat with both hands to touch her but a man's voice said, "No, don't touch her." I immediately pulled my hands back to my chest and realized, "That's right, I don't want to ruin it for her." After awhile, she started to fade away. I felt sad that she was going, and then it was over.

I didn't tell anyone about this until my husband and I were watching a TV show about near-death experiences a month later. I told Bill because my experience was so similar and he felt it was from God. I also eventually told my father. Dad asked me to tell him the story again four times during the week before he passed on even though he wasn't ill and his death was totally unexpected.

Our son Mike was killed in a car accident on January 13, 2001. I can not begin to put into words how difficult that was but the experience I had eleven years ago has helped us through this terrible time. We KNOW Mike is still with us as we have had several contacts from him. We miss Mike's physical presence very much but we have the peace of mind that he is alive and well in another place.

Facilitated ADCs

I was trained by Dr. Raymond Moody to conduct what I call *facilitated after-death contacts*, "FADCs." In the early 1990's, Moody developed this technique as described in his books *Reunions* and *The Last Laugh*. Many grieving persons had told him, 'If I could only talk to my departed loved one again—even for just five minutes. . .' This motivated him to research practical ways to *facilitate* contact with those in spirit world.

FADCs involve *mirror gazing* in a totally quiet and nearly darkened room. Sensory deprivation and the mirror's clear optical depth provide an optimal environment for detecting and communicating with nonphysical beings. As the name implies, this technique attempts to set up or facilitate a meaningful contact with departed loved ones. Perceptions may involve the standard senses of sight, sound, touch and smell or more subtle variations of these such as mind-sight, an inner feeling, and telepathic communication.

Mirror gazing is not new but, rather, has been practiced on every continent over the millennia. One hundred years ago, scientists investigating sightings of ghostly apparitions found they often occurred in mirrors or other reflective surfaces. In 19th century Europe and the U.S., mirror gazing was a popular form of paranormal entertainment. The technique is safe and time-tested; there is no evidence that anyone has ever been harmed by an apparition. (8)

Some people are concerned about Biblical admonitions against consorting with spirits. As always, it's useful to examine such passages in their full context. Warnings such as "Do not resort to ghosts and spirits, nor make yourselves unclean by seeking them out" primarily appear in Leviticus chapters 19 and 20. These 'you shalt not' commandments also warn against planting fields with two kinds of seed, wearing garments with two kinds of yarn, and cutting the hair and beard in a certain way. Do those who bring up Biblical objections to conjuring spirits also take these other instructions seriously?

A number of validation cases have surfaced during FADCs led by therapists around the world. These authenticated cases further add to the depth and breadth of afterlife evidence. On one occasion, several subjects in a large booth saw the same apparition as confirmed by comparing notes afterwards.

During our radio interview, Dr. Moody discussed another validation case: "I have a good friend in France who is well known as a psychologist and journalist. He set up (the booth) for a friend who had lost a loved one and was having a great deal of difficulty about it. He left her in the booth for an hour. When he went in to get her, she waved him away and said, 'No, don't come in now, something is going on.' When he looked up, he saw the apparition too and heard it talking to her. So, yes, once in awhile, the facilitator also sees the apparition." (9)

In the following *group* FADCs, I received information confirming that I was actually in contact with departed souls and not just imagining it. During one session, two other subjects, "Chris and Mary," joined me in the booth. For clinical objectivity, we purposely did not share information about whom we hoped to contact. Twenty minutes into the session, I saw a gauzy female figure forming in the bottom of my peripheral vision. It looked like someone at the halfway stage of getting beamed up on *Star Trek*. First an outline and then the interior partly filled in so that I could actually see the figure of an average height female with long brown hair who appeared to be about thirty-five years-old.

I looked at her directly to see more clearly and the image disappeared. Then I recalled that, like auras, disembodied spirits are best seen with the peripheral vision and that focusing too intently can stop the contact. I relaxed and returned my gaze toward the mirror. Soon the image began forming again and I mentally asked what name she went by. A thought impression of the names 'Mary' and 'Margaret' immediately registered. My ever-active brain complained that I could just be making all this up.

I next silently asked who she came to contact and received the impression that it was for Chris. "Well," my skeptical mind chimed in, "that's a 50-50 chance" since I didn't know the person. Just after that, I felt a distinct and moderately forceful tap on my left shoulder blade—as if Spirit was saying "Uh-huh, are you making that up?!"

Now, I had set up the room and knew that no one else was in there. Through my side-vision, I could see Chris and Mary five feet away so I knew they didn't do it. Several minutes later, I felt another firm tap in the same place and a brisk rubbing along the lateral aspect of my left thigh.

After the session, we shared our experiences. When I told about the names I received and said they were for Chris, she covered her mouth and exclaimed: "Margaret is my mother and Mary is my grandmother!" The combination of seeing a spirit, getting touched three times, and receiving verifiable information that I did not know was, needless to say, potent proof for me and the other participants.

Another group FADC session also resulted in an impressive combination of "hits" or accurate receiving of details that I did not know. Our group of six again did not exchange personal information before the session. As we sat before the mirrors, I heard the name "Jim" almost shouted in my mind. Just after that, I mentally saw a small boat being tossed about on rough seas. Afterwards, as I told about the name, one of the group members, "Jean," exclaimed: "Jim is my father's name and that's who I hoped to contact."

I wasn't so impressed with this since Jim is a common name to which someone in the group would likely have a connection. But when I described the boat scene, Jean's face turned white. "I recently spoke with my sister and told her about this upcoming experience," she shared. "I asked her, 'If I do contact dad, is there anything you want me to ask him?' My sister replied, 'Yes, my husband and I are planning an oceanic sailboat cruise. Ask him if we will be safe.'"

Conclusions and Action Steps

Everyone wants reassurance that they will see departed loved ones again. Paul McCartney, whose wife Linda passed on in 1998, said he's comforted by thoughts that her spirit lives on: "After Linda died, I think all of us in the family would hear noises or see things and think 'That's Linda; that's mom...' And I think in some ways, it's very comforting to think she's still here. . . You don't know if it's true. But it's a great thought. And it's an uplifting thought. So I allow myself to go there." (10)

After-death contacts—whether shared, evidential, transformative, or facilitated—constitute a remarkable body of evidence for the continuation of consciousness after crossing over. These strong indications that we and our loved ones don't really "die", but merely change worlds are immensely comforting and healing. The frequency of these phenomena and the many associated validation aspects further contribute to the evidence that we are, in fact, timeless spiritual beings.

Knowledge followed by action is the best combination for optimal growth so I recommend completing the follow-up exercises for each category of evidence. Suggested action steps for this chapter include:

∞ Recall whether you have experienced any peculiar events—even subtle and fleeting—that may have been attempts by spirit beings to contact you

∞ Ask your family members and friends if they—or anyone they know—have ever experienced an ADC

∞ Reflect upon your feelings about the appropriateness of trying to contact departed spirits

Benefit ∞ 1

Little or no fear and grief about your own "death and dying" and that of your loved ones

Dick, my brother-in-law Jack's father, recently departed. That night, Jack dreamed he saw his dad in a bright, white haze filled hallway. Down the hallway about twenty feet beyond Dick, were many people who Jack immediately recognized as family and friends who had passed away over the years.

Well past them in the distance was a brilliant white light circled in brilliant blue. As Dick moved toward the light, these relatives, friends and his parents were greeting him. Jack also saw two people greeting Dick whom he didn't immediately recognize.

The dream felt so real and so reassuring that Jack was deeply comforted and immediately awakened. He immediately told his wife Nancy about what had happened and shared his vision of all Dick's family and friends greeting him, but especially the two people Jack described that he did not recognize.

The next evening, Nancy received a call from one of Dick's cousins expressing her condolences. She told Nancy that Dick was the third relative who had passed away in the last month and that two other cousins of Dick had gone before him just recently. Jack then immediately realized the two people he did not recognize were cousins of his Dad.

Jack's dream ADC makes him believe his father has passed on to a greater life and was being welcomed to the next part of infinity.

Jack felt doubly reassured when he heard this validation of his "dream."

Dick had been very ill for some time and his death was a blessing. It's never easy when a loved one passes on, no matter what the age, but bereaved loved ones agree that the passing of a child is the toughest test of faith. As such, in this discussion I will focus on children "dying" although these principles apply to those who transition at any age.

Even though "death" seems more timely for a ninety year-old versus a five year-old, it appears that *earth-age* and *soul-age* are quite different. A deceased child's soul might have been more evolved than that of a nonagenarian, thus the abbreviated earth visit. That is, a five-year-old in earth years may be a very old and wise soul, thus his or her brief incarnation. An enlightened perspective reminds us that five or ninety-five earth-years are just a blink of an eye in spirit-time.

The reality of spiritual realms is difficult for some to fathom because the physical world seems so overwhelmingly real. In *How Can I Help?*, Ram Dass and Paul Gorman share a powerfully instructive story about the great Tibetan teacher Marpa: "One day, Marpa's eldest son was killed. Off by himself, alone with his grief, Marpa wept. One of his students approached him and said, 'I don't understand. You teach that all this is illusion, created by the clinging and desire and resistance. Yet here you are weeping. If all this is illusion, why do you grieve so deeply?' Marpa replied, 'Yes, everything here is illusion. And the death of a child is the greatest of these illusions.'" (11)

What a blessing to begin to see through the illusion that physicality is all there is. So many people suffer grievously when their loved ones—especially children—change worlds. While presenting workshops around the country, I've met people with incredibly difficult challenges. For example, one woman in South Carolina had seven pregnancies: of these, four were miscarriages and two died at a young age. She said that she couldn't have survived all that pain without personal faith and knowledge of life after death.

When children pass on, their loved ones have two choices: they can become bitter, lose faith, and use that tragedy to further prove that the world is unjust, chaotic, and Godless. Or, they can use that pain to help others in some way. They can honor the deceased by learning and growing spiritually. They can incorporate the strengths of their departed loved one and apply those spiritual gifts to improve the world. Finally, they can take solace in the evidence that the child's soul was apparently ready to graduate into another realm.

I asked Dr. Wayne Dyer, "What do you tell parents whose little children have passed on?" He answered: "That there is no death, that's not a possibility. We are never born and we never die. Our true essence is that we are spiritual beings having a human experience. When God calls Home young people, they were only here for that amount of time because that's all the time they chose to be here. Self-actualizing people get over death almost as if it didn't happen because for them it doesn't happen. Once you see that, you realize you can never be separate from them. There's a sacred hoop that connects all of us." (12)

These viewpoints are reminiscent of St. Paul's exhortations to remember the good news of our true nature. Then we realize the meaning of I Corinthians 15:55, "O' death, where is thy sting? O' grave, where is thy victory?"

The faith of some people is understandably shaken by apparent tragedies such as the death of children. Knowledge of our soul natures helps explain these great challenges in several ways. Short earthly lives are called 'filler' incarnations and may be designed primarily to help others learn lessons. Even brief visits by a soul can nonetheless deeply touch many hearts and open minds. I know several cases in which families were brought closer together and onto the spiritual path after a little one changed worlds. Finally, remember that we will be with loved ones who have crossed over in a relatively short time.

Some people wonder how Divine perfection can be true when mass deaths and large scale disasters occur. Based on his spiritual regression research, Michael Newton, Ph.D., says, "I have found that souls essentially *volunteer* in advance for bodies that will have sudden fatal illnesses, are to be killed by someone, or come to an abrupt end of life with many others from a catastrophic event. Souls who become involved in these tragedies are not caught in the wrong place at the wrong time with a capricious God looking the other way. Every soul has a motive for the events in which it chooses to participate." (13)

From an earthly perspective, such events appear to be tragedies; from a spiritual perspective, they are simply *exit opportunities* for souls who are ready to move on.

One final note. Some want to communicate with their departed loved ones, know what their life on the other side is like, and so on. This interest is healthy to a point and can help strengthen ones faith. An *excessive focus* on this, however, can detract from living fully now and perhaps hamper those in spirit from doing the same. A preoccupation with these concerns also suggests fear about death, not faith about afterlife. An informed understanding that you will see them again lends a peace about living in the now and trusting how the future will unfold.

Evidence Category 2

Near-death Experiences

When I was nine years old, my uncle Cliff's car collided with a semi. He nearly died from severe multiple injuries and was in the hospital for a long time. When he finally came home, he was pale, thin, missing teeth, and couldn't walk. From his hospital bed in their living room, he spoke through a wired jaw about what he experienced when he almost died. Walking in a meadow of lush green grass, hearing beautiful music, and seeing Jesus. Feeling an accelerated awareness with everything being more brilliant and colorful than usual. No longer fearing death. Being so peaceful that, except for missing his family, he didn't care if he came back.

Since then, many near-death experiences have provided impressive evidence for the continuation of consciousness beyond the grave. That many of these cases have been validated by respected scientists further points to the authenticity of nonphysical realities. The abbreviation for near-death experiences is NDE; the plural is NDEs and those who experience these states are termed NDErs.

Tens of thousands of NDE cases, many of them documented by doctors and scientists, have demonstrated the persistence of awareness after "death." Typical stages during a NDE include: being out of the body, hearing a buzzing or ringing sound, going through a tunnel, seeing radiant light, meeting departed loved ones and spiritual beings, sensing beautiful scenes and colors, hearing angelic music, feeling peaceful and at home, learning lessons, being told it's not ones time to stay on the other side, and a rapid journey back into the successfully resuscitated body.

Although NDEs were first described thousands of years ago, they are much more common now because of advances in medical resuscitative capabilities. Many more people are now successfully brought back from the brink of *biological* or irreversible death. These NDErs were temporarily *clinically dead*, that is, had cessation of their heart, lung, and/or brain functions. During that time, a significant percentage of them have fascinating and life-changing experiences.

Clinical reports of near-death experiences first came to my attention when I was working as a respiratory therapist and attending theology school. While the topic of NDEs was sometimes met with skepticism by health care professionals, my earlier experience with uncle Cliff helped me keep an open mind. I interviewed a number of patients who were successfully resuscitated and asked them: "Do you remember anything during your time while unconscious?" Several excitedly told me about beatific experiences with classic NDE traits.

In 1982, pollster George Gallup, Jr., found that eight million adults in the United States have had a NDE or out-of-body experience (OBE) which I'll discuss later. This high incidence and the immense amount of validated research on NDEs constitute the most impressive evidence indicating life after death. Taken together with the other categories, NDEs are the 'final straw' that convince many people that our real selves do not die.

I have categorized NDE information into the following groups: historical continuity, verifiable cases, pediatric validation cases, life previews, out-of-body experiences, empathetic NDEs, blind persons and NDEs, and transformative aspects.

Historical Continuity

NDEs have been reported independently across time in various cultures, a fact that further increases the credibility of this phenomenon. They were first reported thousands of years ago, as described in *The Tibetan Book of the Dead*, *The Egyptian Book of the Dead*, and *The Aztec Song of the Dead*. These descriptions were lost or little known for centuries yet score remarkably high on modern NDE measures such as the "Near-Death Experience Validity Scale" by Ken Ring, Ph.D. Their reports of what souls encounter after death also mirror those of other cultures and transcendent episodes experienced via consciousness altering substances.

In *The Light Beyond*, Dr. Raymond Moody states that there have been cases of NDEs far back in history, dating to references by Greek philosopher Plato in 347 B.C. Pope Gregory the Great's sixth-century *Dialogues* are a set of deathbed visions, ghost stories and near-death accounts providing evidence of the soul's immortality. Dr. Carol Zaleski, author of *Otherworld Journeys*, says the literature of the Middle Ages is filled with such accounts. (1)

A massive amount of NDE literature exists thanks to Moody, Ring, Greyson, Morse, Grof, Sabom, Grosso, Ritchie, Lundahl, Osis, Haraldsson, Wade, Tart, Atwater, Cooper, Becker and others. Current studies of diverse age groups in other cultures show the same patterns or universality of reports. Research findings lead to many questions such as: What is the nature of this consciousness? How can accurate awareness be explained when people are nearly dead, blind, or unconscious? And, since this consciousness exists during at least part of the dying process, does it exist after actual bodily death?

Verifiable Cases

NDE evidence with verifiable aspects strongly points to the existence of awareness surviving physical death. In *Lessons from the Light*, Ken Ring, Ph.D., says that many people ". . . tell of leaving their bodies for a moment and having a panoramic and detailed perception of the environment around their body. Suppose, then, these descriptions could be checked independently and verified. If one could show that these patients could not possibly have seen what they did naturally or acquired this information by other means, we would have some fairly impressive evidence to support the objectivity of NDEs."

Much research has been done and the vote is in. As Ring concludes, "We now have good evidence, and from multiple sources, that the NDE is indeed an experience that has its own objective character and is, in a phrase, 'on the level.' (After considering evidentiary cases) I hope you will be reassured that the doubts about the validity of the NDE can be safely dispatched on purely scientific grounds." (2)

In *Messages from the Masters*, Brian Weiss, M.D., describes a number of NDEs with verifiable aspects. One woman suffered massive head trauma from a severe auto accident and was very near death. As the doctor spoke with the family about the inevitably fatal outcome, the patient floated out of her body. She found her family even though the conference was far from where the medical team was working on her. Upon overhearing the conversation, she tried to communicate that she wasn't dead. After her recovery, she accurately repeated the conversation between the surgeon and her family.

Another patient awoke in a very agitated state after major surgery. During the procedure, she floated above her body when her blood pressure and heart rhythm became abnormal. From this vantage point, she could see the surgeons and read the anesthesiologist's notes in her chart. Upon awakening in the recovery room, she was still panicked because of these complications. She correctly told Dr. Weiss what had been written on her chart even though she had been unconscious. Because of the positioning of her body and the doctor's, she couldn't have seen the notes even if she had been awake.

Dr. Weiss concludes, "I have heard these and other stories of clinical accounts of patients with near-death and out-of-body experiences from so many physicians that I cannot explain them away on medical or physiological grounds." (3)

There are so many validated NDE cases that they are collectively known as 'tennis shoe stories.' In *Closer To The Light*, Melvin Morse, M.D., and Paul Perry describe the story of psychologist Kim Clark who was counseling a patient named Maria after she had a cardiac arrest. They state, "The woman wasn't interested in what Clark had to say. Instead, she wanted to talk about how she had floated around the hospital while doctors struggled to start her heart. To prove that she had left her body, the woman insisted that there was a shoe on the ledge outside Clark's window. Clark opened the window, but could see no shoe. 'It's out there,' the woman insisted. Clark leaned out, but still could not see the shoe. 'It's around the corner,' said the woman. Courageously, Clark crawled onto the ledge of her fifth-floor window and around the corner. There sat a shoe, just as Maria had described." (4)

The NDE literature is also full of accounts of survivors who, while clinically dead, encountered departed relatives who were unknown to the subject during life. Later, positive identification was confirmed by photographic or anecdotal evidence. In addition, many patients develop extrasensory abilities during and after the NDE.

Another verifying aspect involves so-called "surprise" meetings on the other side with people the survivor didn't know had died. For example, one woman was very ill at the same time that her sister was near death on a different floor of the same hospital. During her NDE, the woman watched from above the resuscitative efforts on her body. To her surprise, she met her sister and they enjoyed a great conversation until the sister began moving away from her.

The woman states, "I tried to go with her, but she kept telling me to stay where I was. 'It's not your time,' she said . . . Then she just began to recede off into the distance through a tunnel while I was left there alone. When I awoke, I told the doctor that my sister had died. He denied it, but at my insistence, he had a nurse check on it. She had in fact died, just as I knew she did." (5)

In *Transformed By The Light*, Morse and Perry relate a similar case of a woman who was bleeding profusely after delivery a baby. As medical personnel worked on her, she could see them from a vantage point above and her intense pain suddenly disappeared. She went through a tunnel toward bright light but before she reached the end, "A gentle voice told me I had to go back. Then I met a dear friend, a neighbor from a town that we had left. He also told me to go back. I hit the hospital bed with an electrifying jerk and the pain was back. I was being rushed into an operating theater for surgery to stop the bleeding. It was three weeks later that my husband decided I was well enough to be told that my dear friend in that other town had died in an accident on the day my daughter was born." (6)

Pediatric Validation Cases

Young children, who describe the sequence of events during NDEs just as adults do, provide an especially impressive category of evidence. The literature is rich with verifiable accounts of pediatric NDEs that include many complex details about resuscitative procedures that are incomprehensible to young children. Children have not been exposed to religious or cultural views about what happens after death. They tend to view death as a vacation and something the departed will return from.

Two examples of pediatric NDE cases are described in *Closer to the Light* by Melvin Morse, M.D., and Paul Perry. The first involved an eight-year-old boy who fell from a bridge and hit his head on a rock in the water. After floating face down for at least five minutes, he was pulled from the water by a policeman. The boy had stopped breathing and didn't have a pulse; after performing CPR for thirty minutes, the policeman declared him dead. Even so, a helicopter emergency team started resuscitation and rushed him to the hospital. The boy didn't regain consciousness until two days later when he accurately described his rescue and resuscitation in great detail. He knew all of this, he said, because he had been watching the whole time from outside his body.

The second case involved a NDE *at age nine months*; Mark told his parents about this experience at age three. His parents had never told him about his cardiac arrest and most children don't remember events at that age. "Then, following a Christmas pageant, he said that God didn't look like the man in the play they had just seen. When his father asked him what he meant, Mark told him what had happened during that frantic night two years earlier: 'I saw nurses and doctors standing over me trying to wake me up. I flew out of the room and (went to the waiting room, where I) saw Grandpa and Grandma crying and holding each other. I think they thought I was going to die. He then reported seeing a long, dark tunnel and crawling up it."

The bright light at the end of the tunnel kept him going and he found 'a bright place' where he 'ran through the fields with God.' "He was very animated when he described this run with God. He said that one 'can double jump in Heaven'. . . God then asked if he wanted to go 'back home.' Mark said 'no,' but God told him he would come back again some other day." Mark vividly remembered his experience until age five and, at the time Morse wrote the book, was a well-adjusted teenager. (7)

Life Previews

NDEs occasionally provide glimpses into the future as well. These so-called *life preview experiences* provide another validation aspect since, in a number of cases, the events foreseen did come true.

Dr. Moody describes a personal encounter with a woman who had a life preview during her NDE in 1971. In 1975, several months before the publication of *Life After Life*, Moody's children were trick-or-treating at Halloween. A friendly couple asked the children's names; when the oldest said, 'Raymond Avery Moody,' the woman looked startled and said to Mrs. Moody, 'I must talk to your husband.'

Moody states: "When I spoke to this woman later on, she told me about her NDE in 1971. She'd had heart failure and lung collapse during surgery and had been clinically dead for a long time. During this experience, she met a guide who took her through a life review and gave her information about the future. Toward the end of the experience, she was shown a picture of me, given my full name, and told that 'when the time was right,' she would tell me her story. I found this encounter remarkable."(8)

Psychiatrist Bruce Greyson, M.D., states that about one-third of those recalling a life review had visions of personal future events. Dr. Ring reports several life preview cases in his books *Heading Toward Omega* and *Lessons from the Light*, including the following one.

One NDE survivor, Nel, found herself looking at a giant television screen during her life review. She made a conscious decision to return to her physical body but just then a second TV screen showed her glimpses of what was to come: a prolonged period of pain; family members who would suffer physical pain; a sister-in-law who would die prematurely. Dr. Ring, who has known Nel for more than fifteen years, is convinced that the events she foresaw during her NDE did indeed take place, just as she was shown. (9)

Out-of-Body Experiences

The term *out-of-body experience* (OBE) usually refers to a person's awareness leaving the body without being clinically dead. OBEs sometimes happen spontaneously during meditative states; the phenomenon of 'astral travel' is one such example of an OBE. Intense experiences, for example, childbirth or being in imminent danger, can also trigger OBEs. In the past, people often kept such occurrences to themselves for fear of being considered crazy. As such, the frequency of OBEs is likely much greater than has been reported.

A ten-year-old girl who attended one of my workshops with her mother described an OBE she had at age two. Her mom left her with a baby-sitter for the first time ever and gave clear instructions to attend to the baby if she cried. The baby-sitter, however, had his own ideas about child rearing and ignored the infant when she cried. Receiving no comfort from her mother for the first time, the little one cried and cried until she experienced a strange event.

Even though she couldn't see out the window from her crib, she could see another version of herself on the sidewalk below. This 'other self' reassured her and told her it would be OK. The infant's OBE continued as her awareness floated out into the living room and saw the baby sitter there. She remembers the clothing she had on and the appearance of the sitter. Her mother verified the facts as told by this youngster who is wise beyond her years.

An OBE verified by physical evidence occurred with Robert Monroe who wrote *Journeys Out of The Body*. Monroe discovered his ability to travel out of his physical body and wanted to non-physically visit a co-worker who was vacationing in New Jersey. As told by attorney Sidney Freeman in *Life After Death*:

He wanted her to remember the 'visit' so he said he was going to pinch her. 'Oh, you don't need to do that, I'll remember' she replied mentally. Nevertheless, he pinched her—in the side, just above the hips. He tried to do it gently. She screamed, 'Ow.' That Tuesday they were both back at work. Did she remember the 'visit,' he asked. No, she said.

Did she remember the pinch? 'Was that you?' she replied. 'I was sitting there, talking to the girls when all of a sudden I felt this terrible pinch. I must have jumped a foot. I thought my brother-in-law had come back and sneaked up behind me. I turned around but there was no one there. I never had any idea it was you!' They went into his private office. She lifted her sweater slightly above her skirt. *There were two brown and blue marks at exactly the spot where he had pinched her.* He apologized for hurting her. He thought he had done it gently and said he wouldn't do it again. This remarkable incident showed a *physical effect* from an out-of-body visit. (10)

In 1974, I experienced a profound OBE during meditation while lying on the grass on a warm spring day. After about twenty minutes, I felt as if my body was becoming part of the earth. I couldn't feel my arms or legs and felt like my consciousness was several miles up in the sky. At that moment, my fear of death and change decreased dramatically. I felt totally assured that there is a spiritual reality that renders physical change relatively meaningless. Over thirty years later, the memory of that experience is still clear and inspiring.

Empathetic Near-Death Experiences

Another aspect of NDE evidence is the *empathetic or shared* near-death experience. In these cases, loved ones or health care providers themselves have other-worldly experiences when someone passes on.

Joan Borysenko, Ph.D., relates a beautiful empathetic NDE that occurred at the moment of her mother's passing. Her mother had long been cynical about and critical of Joan's spiritual work. Joan and her son Justin were present as her mom passed over. At that moment, the room was filled with light and both realized what Justin verbalized: "I feel like Grandma is holding the door to eternity open to give us a glimpse. Can you feel it? You must be so grateful to your mother. You know, she was a very great soul. And she embodied to take a role that was much smaller than the wisdom in her soul and she did it as a gift for you so that you'd have something to resist against." (11)

Why are such reports surfacing more now? There is a greater societal openness to these topics, especially among baby-boomers, whose parents are aging and dying. Hospital visitation policies have changed and more family members are present during the death of loved ones and thus can potentially experience empathetic NDEs. Finally, improvements in pain medications now allow dying persons to enjoy more clarity just before crossing over.

"Sue" recently had a psycho-spiritual session with me during which, while under hypnosis, she visualized a healing trip to spirit side. She emailed me the next day with this message:

After I left our session Saturday, I felt wonderfully different; there are no words I can use to sufficiently describe it. My mother called me at midnight and told me my grandmother was not doing very well. Grandma and I have always been very close and I've often thought we were soul mates. We stayed with her through the night and called the emergency squad around 4:30 A.M.

At the hospital, I was with her praying, holding her hand, and encouraging her to follow the Light. At 2 P.M. Sunday, the most beautiful flash of indescribable love and light encompassed and overwhelmed me totally. I literally cried out, "Grandma, it is so beautiful!" She took her last breath immediately after that. It was absolutely amazing. I remember having that feeling during our session, only it wasn't as intense.

In *The Last Laugh*, Dr. Moody discusses reports of empathetic NDEs: "Dozens upon dozens of first-rate individuals have related to me that, as a loved one died, they themselves lifted out of their own bodies and accompanied their dying loved ones upward toward a beautiful and loving light. Others have said that, as they sat with their dying loved ones, they perceived deceased relatives coming to greet the one who was passing away. . . Lots of doctors and nurses have described to me how they perceived patients' spirits leaving their bodies at the point of death." (12)

I experienced this phenomenon firsthand many years ago while working in hospitals. I was usually assigned to the emergency room and intensive care units where I assisted during many resuscitations. In those days, dying patients seldom received conscious attention to their emotional and spiritual needs. So while working with critically ill patients, I spoke directly into their ears, reassured them that everything possible was being done, and encouraged them to trust God. On several occasions, I saw a faint white light emanate from the patient's chest region just before the time of physical death was announced. Looking back, it seems that my empathy for those in transition may have enabled these sixth sense experiences that I revere to this day.

A fascinating variation of an empathetic NDE was relayed to me by several people in England. An older woman passed on and, after her funeral, the family was gathered for dinner with fifteen close family members. The widower's head slumped down during dinner and the family assumed he had fallen asleep after several long and difficult days. After several minutes, someone became concerned and checked on him but found no sign of breathing or heartbeat.

They called their neighbor who was a doctor and she came right over. The doctor verified the absence of vital signs, now eight or nine minutes since the widower had slumped over.

She asked the family if they would like her to try and 'bring him back', at which time a distraught female family member let out a loud wail of despair. At that, the old man immediately jolted back to life. He said that he just had to go make sure his wife had made it over OK because she was no good at finding her way anywhere on her own. He would not be staying 'there', he commented, because he still had too much to do 'here'. He was taken to the hospital by ambulance where no sign of any health problem could be detected. Since then, he seems to have taken a new lease on life and has been energetic and healthy.

Blind Persons and NDEs

NDEs reported by those who are blind constitute particularly impressive evidence for a continuation of consciousness beyond physical death. In *Books of the Dead*, Stan Grof, M.D., discusses, ". . . reported cases where individuals, who were blind because of medically confirmed organic damage to their optical system, could at the time of clinical death see the environment. . . Occurrences of this kind, unlike most of the other aspects of near-death phenomena, can be subjected to objective verification. They thus represent the most convincing proof that what happens in near-death experiences is more than the hallucinatory phantasmagoria of physiologically impaired brains." [13]

As amazing as verifiable NDEs are, they are even more astonishing when the subjects are blind. In the foreword of *Mindsight* by Ken Ring, Ph.D., and Sharon Cooper, Ph.D., researcher Charles T. Tart, Ph.D., states, "The authors of this book have practiced essential science, real science. They have looked at the facts about NDEs, particularly NDEs among the blind, and provided us with extremely stimulating and thought-provoking material that we must take into account in coming to terms with reality . . . these facts argue strongly that there is some very real sense in which we are 'spiritual' beings, not just material beings." [14]

Ring and Cooper provide an example of a validation NDE in a blind person. Irreversibly blinded earlier in the day after a surgical accident, Nancy later went into respiratory arrest and was unconscious. As the hospital staff wheeled her down the hall, her gurney hit the elevator. At that moment, Nancy describes stepping out of herself and watching the events around her. She looked down the hall about twenty feet and saw two men standing there, her son's father and her boyfriend. Then she looked down at her body still laying on the gurney.

She saw the IV, black ambu bag covering her face, the surgical head cover on her, white sheets, and three staff people on her left and right. At that point, Nancy says, "And then the classic white light, bright, the most beautiful light, soothing, comforting just washing over (me)."

Afterwards, interviews with her boyfriend and ex-husband corroborated the details outside the elevator. The positions of the ambu bag and staff members would have blocked her from seeing the two men and other details. Of this, Ring and Cooper state, "Thus, we conclude that in all probability there was no possibility for Nancy to see what she did with her physical eyes. . . . Yet, she did see, and, as the corroborative testimony we have provided shows, she apparently saw truly. . . . There is no question that NDEs in the blind do occur and, furthermore, that they take the same general form and are comprised of the very same elements that define the NDEs of sighted individuals." (15)

In my radio interview with Dr. Ring, he added that a panel of vision specialists was not able to come up with alternative medical explanations that could explain these findings. This research, he stated, makes a very strong supportive argument for the religious and spiritual beliefs of many people about the existence of afterlife.

Transformative Aspects

A common and enduring aspect of NDEs is the accompanying transformative effect. NDErs have such a strong belief in afterlife that any fear of death is nearly or completely extinguished. Survivors of NDEs typically reorder their life priorities and often change to more meaningful jobs involving service to others. They also view their bodies as vehicles for their souls and take better care of themselves.

My good friend Ed had a NDE after open heart surgery. At bedtime on his first day home from the hospital, his dimly lit room filled with bright light and he felt more energetic, joyful, and peaceful than he ever had in his life. He was given the choice to cross over or remain on earth. He decided to stay. As soon as he made this choice, the light subsided and he was back in a painful post-operative state. But his life is now radically different. He knows—without a doubt—that he can't lose: if he lives to one hundred years of age, that's great; if he dies today, he gets to resume the wonderful journey he glimpsed.

A deep faith and internalized belief about God and afterlife are common after NDEs. These dramatic lessons impart a lasting hope and assurance of things not seen but nevertheless vitally real. Says Nancy Bush, past-president of the International Association for Near-Death Studies, "Most near-death survivors say they don't think there is a God. They know."

A *U.S. News & World Report* article stated, "No matter what the nature of the (near-death) experience, it alters some lives. Alcoholics find themselves unable to imbibe. Hardened criminals opt for a life of helping others. Atheists embrace the existence of a deity, while dogmatic members of a particular religion report feeling welcome in any church or temple or mosque." Further, those who had undergone NDEs became more altruistic, less materialistic, and more loving. Having stared eternity in the face, people returning from NDEs often lose their taste for ego-boosting achievement. (16)

Such positive transformations also occur in children. Studies that track pediatric NDErs show that they are happier, have less drug use, enjoy better relationships, and in general are more hopeful than those around them. Their glimpse of the Light and life beyond apparently affects them for the better throughout their lives.

Even when there is orthodox religious training to the contrary, NDErs do not describe death as an end, or an entry into either a fiery hell or golden streets. Instead, they commonly describe dying as a transition, an entry into a higher state of consciousness. Other comparisons are to a reunion, homecoming, awakening, graduating, or escaping from jail. They don't view God as a punishing, judgmental despot but, rather, a totally fair and loving Presence that works with each soul no matter how sinful or awful their deeds while on earth.

Changes in spiritual views happen to nonbelievers in God and the hereafter just as frequently as to believers. After a NDE, most everyone becomes more spiritually oriented. They have learned that an emphasis on loving compassion —not doctrines and denominations— is most important and that the Light is all-encompassing.

NDEs usually engender more enlightened theological views. Having glimpsed the Light, these near-death survivors know firsthand that the Creator *completely and always* forgives and understands. They have experienced an almost unbearable degree of love and acceptance and know that the Infinite is not vengeful and judgmental. Most NDErs no longer fear eternal punishment in hell, nor believe any such place exists.

Moody states, "One NDEer I spoke to had been a minister of the fire and brimstone variety. It wasn't infrequent, he said, for him to tell his congregation that if they didn't believe the Bible in a certain way, they would be condemned to burn eternally. When he went through his NDE, he said the being of light told him not to speak to his congregation like this anymore. But it was done in a nondemanding way. The being just implied that what he was doing was making the lives of his congregation miserable. When this preacher returned to the pulpit, he did so with a message of love, not fear." (17)

NDErs are usually affirmative on the question of *universal salvation,* that is, a never-ending opportunity for a heavenly afterlife *for all.* Some people question whether the Light embraces *everyone,* especially those committing morally reprehensible acts like rape, murder, and molestation. Dr. Ring states that the answer by NDErs is unqualified: everyone gets to enter the Light. This runs counter to some teachings and some question, "Even Hitler?"

Of this, Ring states, "I remember an answer that was given to this query by an NDEr friend of mine who, as a child, had suffered severe sexual and physical abuse from her father. When she found herself in the Light, she asked it telepathically, 'Does everyone come here?' She was told 'Yes.' Then, she herself asked the very question that represents the limit for most people: 'Even Hitler?' 'Yes.' And, then, pushing the Light even further, she found herself asking, 'Even my father?' Again, 'Yes.'" (18)

Conclusions and Action Steps

The existing NDE research successfully refutes skeptics who claim that NDEs can be explained solely by physiological changes such as lack of oxygen. Likewise, various aspects of NDEs, such as verified vision by blind persons, cannot be satisfactorily explained by psychological dynamics. The evidence in this section is very difficult to explain unless there is indeed a transcendent component to the human experience.

Suggested action steps include:

∞ Read and study further about this topic

∞ Ask your family, friends, and coworkers if they, or anyone they know, have had a NDE

∞ If possible, talk to someone who has personally undergone a NDE

∞ Reflect about how this information affects your belief in afterlife and spiritual realities

Benefit ∞ 2

Greater trust about all the rhythms of life, even those involving suffering and tragedy

Illness, disability, broken relationships, financial loss, unhappy or nonexistent jobs, unfulfilled dreams, cruelty, and injustice. At times, they are part and parcel of life. And that doesn't include your own death nor that of your family and friends—which we already discussed. Nor does it include life's inevitable changes like aging and others—which we'll discuss later.

My younger daughter recently graduated from high school. One after another, the smiling students received their diplomas, exuberant about finishing their lessons.

I knew the inside story of some of these students. There was Melinda, whose mother crossed over a few years ago after a rare infection. Chad, whose father recently passed on after a heart attack. Megan, just out of the hospital after exploratory surgery and a possible battle with cancer ahead.

There was Brandi, whose parents divorced when she was little, and Ruth, whose parents are waiting until the graduation parties are over to separate. Tom was adopted and never knew his biological parents.

Amy, who is wheelchair bound because of spina bifida, had to be pushed across the rough ground at this outdoor graduation. During the ceremony, she glanced down at her pale shriveled legs several times and covered them with her gown—maybe to shield them from the sun, maybe out of self-consciousness.

Welcome to life on planet earth. So difficult and scary. So rich, so bittersweet, so full of challenging experiences. So full of growth and service opportunities—especially when confronted with suffering and tragedy.

I discuss life's challenges in an attempt to help those who are suffering to see past the pain. These difficulties can become blessings for those who look for them. As the saying goes, 'When one doors closes, another opens—but it can be hell in the hallway for awhile!' Growth through adversity is not easy but it's possible. To enjoy totally successful lives, we need to remember that change does not equal loss.

In the last thirty-three years of serving many thousands of people in hospitals, mental health centers, and private practice, I've seen an immense amount of hardship. We understandably ask: "Why is there so much suffering?"

Here's a few general comments on this big "why" question, whether the suffering occurs with a broken relationship, unfulfilled dreams, a deformity or illness, or . . .

In answer to the question about why there is so much suffering in life, the Buddha answered, "It's none of your business." Chew on that one for awhile and don't forget your sense of humor.

His comment addresses the fact that life is full of mystery and a spiritually awakening person wouldn't have it any other way. Struggling with the unknown is part of what draws souls to this physical dimension. We grow the most quickly and deeply when our lives aren't working, when we're at rock bottom, when the crap hits the fan. That's when we ask important questions and search for answers.

Realize that time isn't absolutely real and is only a human construct. Our lives on earth, long as they might seem at times, are only a blink of an eye in the span of eternity. So remember that your suffering is time limited and only for awhile.

Then recall that we each really are timeless beings of energy. Our real selves don't and can't die. Yes, I know that it doesn't appear that way from a human perspective. Consider that the sun also appears to disappear when it sets; our spiritual selves continue on after physical death just as surely as the sun will rise tomorrow.

Finally, consider the possibility that you—as a soul—chose life's biggest challenges as a way to increasingly grow, serve, and experience life fully. Much evidence suggests this is so. As such, why not embrace all of life's lessons—not just the easy or fun ones—with faith, courage, and style?

It appears that souls purposely choose life experiences that include probable difficult events. Adventurous souls welcome these opportunities for growth and service to others. Reports from Spirit side say there is a waiting list for souls who want to incarnate on earth because of the powerful potential for rapid growth here.

By the way, there are more peaceful and flowing ways than suffering to learn. We do not have to suffer once important lessons are learned. Some evidence suggests, however, that we—as souls—sign up for advanced curricula knowing that great challenges lie ahead. Souls may *voluntarily* choose major life events—even suffering and tragedy—for the accompanying spiritual growth.

For those who suffer with physical challenges—disabilities, deformities, and serious illness—diverse evidence indicates that we also choose these for a reason. The trials associated with bodily impediments accelerate soul advancement. They also provide excellent opportunities for serving others and glorifying Creator. The same is true for any kind of abuse, mental disorder, or trauma.

Being more accepting and peaceful about the difficult events in life allows us to better learn the accompanying lessons. Yes, set goals and have dreams by all means. But when different outcomes occur, be flexible and trusting enough to roll with the punches and keep an eye upon for the hidden blessings.

Life is exquisitely designed to deliver just what we need for optimal spiritual growth, not what our egos want. This wisdom is reflected in the statement, 'Thy will, not mine, oh Lord.' A spiritually awakening person acknowledges that there is a greater wisdom and order operative in the universe—even in the midst of tragedy.

I know it's easier said than done but it can be done. We're not alone. A magnificent Love, Power, and Intelligence literally guides and assists us each throughout eternity.

One suggestion is to daily pray for clarity, peace, and courage. Then sit quietly for fifteen minutes, breathe slowly and deeply, and listen with your heart. Over time, you'll find that the answers you seek are within and within reach when you quiet the frantic brain.

To paraphrase a line from "A Course in Miracles", you will never fear again when you remember who you are and Who it is that walks beside/within you.

May this evidence enlighten and lighten today and every day as you sojourn through eternity: a spiritual entity having a variety of experiences—some fun, some not so fun—but all important. May you always deeply know that someday, just like nine month old Mark who nearly died, you will run through the fields with God and can even double jump!

Miraculous And Revelatory Experiences

A police officer was directing traffic and had just signaled oncoming cars to stop. He kept his hand up and glanced away for a moment. When he looked back, a large car was still coming very fast and screeching its brakes. With the car now only feet away from him, he realized it wouldn't be able to stop in time and he murmured, "God help me!" The next thing he knew, he was getting up off the sidewalk several lanes of traffic away. Yet he received no injuries, or bruises at all, and no one saw him fly through the air or land.

It was just an immediate change of location.

The man who experienced this miracle told my workshop group: "Before this happened, I really didn't believe in God and all that stuff. I don't know exactly what happened that day, but I've been a firm believer ever since."

Miraculous stories engender feelings of peace and faith—a remembrance that, despite outward appearances to the contrary, everything will make sense someday. They help us remember that we are, first and foremost, spiritual beings having a physical experience.

When we really open our eyes, ears, hearts and minds, we realize firsthand just how many miracles abound. For example, consider the emergence of a mighty oak from an acorn, a fully formed baby nine months after two cells join, and nature's spring renewal. Every aspect of life is unbelievably miraculous but that's not enough for some doubting Thomases. So, periodically, really impressive miracles happen that invoke reverence about the magnificence of creation.

Saint Augustine said, "Miracles do not happen in contradiction to nature, but only in contradiction to that which is known to us of nature." This view is echoed by scientist and former astronaut Dr. Edgar Mitchell who stated, "There are no unnatural or supernatural phenomena, only very large gaps in our knowledge of what is natural . . . We should strive to fill those gaps of ignorance."

Throughout my life, I have been blessed with various revelatory experiences. At age five, my parents showed me a beautiful sunset and I told them "it reminded me of God." I wasn't told about this until I attended theology school many years later. My parents knew of no teaching at home or our church that would cause me to associate God with a sunset. Maybe I retained some memory of our Source.

At age twelve, I was sitting by myself reading the obituary of a prominent man who had just died. As I looked up, light refracted through our beveled glass windows and I went into a deep reverie. A calm loving voice or thought said, "You too will die someday, Mark. What will you do with your life in the meantime? Will you leave this world a better place or will you just take up space?" These and other experiences have motivated me to study soul and afterlife issues.

Open-minded skepticism is healthy but excessive doubt can block appreciation of special lessons in life. Some people have experienced miracles, or at minor ones, but doubt their senses and dismiss them as aberrations of perception. Experiences with a different time-space orientation than usual may initially seem surreal or imaginative, and perhaps even more so as time passes.

Others may discount personal miracles that are more subtle and fleeting than expected. I believe that we would be more aware of life's miracles if we prayed for and were open to them. The incidence of sacred encounters might be increased by regularly enjoying quiet time to meditate, worship, serve others, study spirituality, and commune with nature.

Angel Encounters

Angel encounters are fairly common miracles that indicate life exists beyond just this physical dimension. Numerous authors, poets, artists and visionaries have reported angelic visitations. Many books and documentaries have described angel experiences by people from all walks of life. As with NDEs, the greatest proof is the sheer number of such encounters, especially those that are confirmatory in nature.

One story involving young Marilyn MacDonald was told by Sophy Burnham in *A Book of Angels*. After being dropped off at school by her parents, "Marilyn had darted in front of a car and been hit and tossed high in the air. Her parents watched helplessly as she hit the pavement and rolled over and over toward a large, uncovered, open sewer. But instead of falling in, as expected, she suddenly stopped, right at the lip of the sewer. The parents told this story to the doctor, and they all shook their heads in amazement. How could the child have stopped so suddenly, at the very edge of the sewer, when she had been rolling so fast? In a voice filled with surprise, Marilyn spoke up from the sofa and said, 'But didn't you see that huge, beautiful angel standing in the sewer, holding up her hands to keep me from rolling in?'" (1)

Such interventions are described in scriptures of all religions. The Jewish Kabbalah says there are 49 million angels. The Koran speaks of angels wafting down by the grace of their Lord. In the Bible, Psalms 91 states, "He shall give his angels charge over thee, to keep thee in all thy ways. They shall bear thee up in their hands, lest thou dash thy foot against a stone." Or, apparently, a storm sewer.

Angels are part of Christianity, Judaism, Islam, Buddhism, Taoism, Hinduism, and Zoroastrianism. Ancient Assyrian, Mesopotamian, Viking, and Greek cultures recognized angels as have, in some form or another, all cultures throughout the world. Dante, Milton, Goethe, Swedenborg, and Steiner had angel visions. More recently, such varying personages as George Washington, Carl Jung and Johnny Cash have reported seeing angels.

Accounts of angel visitations often include comforting messages that our true essence is spirit, we do not die, and we will see our loved ones again. Such reassurances remind us how much we are beloved by and watched over by God and the Heavenly Host.

Many dying children see angels. Burnham reports one little boy near "death" who comforted his mother and said, "Don't cry. Do you see my angel out the window? She's telling me I am going fishing." Now why and how would a child in that condition make that up?

A wealth of evidence indicates that we are always ministered to by angels, especially during tragedies. Some people don't believe in angelic assistance because the obvious question inevitably arises, `If angels assist some people, why don't they help everyone in distress?' My understanding regarding this excellent question includes:

♦ Angels do not impose their will on others. If people make poor decisions, that's their choice.

♦ We first need to ask for assistance, and then realize it may not always arrive how, when, and where we expect it.

♦ We will never know how often we are helped. Assistance may be subtle, undetectable, and preventive.

♦ Souls may have chosen significant challenges to assist spiritual growth and angels wouldn't interfere with this plan.

♦ This planet is designed to be a place of intense learning. If the Heavenly Host intervened and prevented all suffering, some of the earthly curriculum would be omitted.

I believe that I experienced the grace and beauty of an angel's visit as I was completing my first book. While writing early one morning, I was looking for a Biblical quote and couldn't find any *Concordance* references. I suddenly felt ecstatic for no apparent reason and heard a slight rustling. Through my peripheral vision, I saw a white gauzy form like the fine lace-work of a wedding dress but as I turned to see it more clearly, it was gone. I felt energized and interpreted this as a sign that my work was in flow with Divine will and my soul's missions. Immediately afterwards, I opened the Bible to the exact page I needed and my eyes went directly to the verses I sought: Hebrews 2:6-7 states, "What is man, that thou art mindful of him? . . . Thou madest him a little lower than the angels…"

The book, *Angels: The Mysterious Messengers* by Rex Hauck, interviews leading thinkers and spiritual leaders on the subject. Interspersed throughout are documented stories of angel encounters. A documentary by the same name was hosted by Patty Duke and produced by American Artists Film Corporation. This film examines the history of angels in ancient and modern times and shares nine real life stories of people whose lives were touched by angels.

My dad experienced what he considered to be angelic visits after his heart by-pass surgery in 2001. On several occasions, he became very cold, but was so sore and tired that pulling up the blankets was difficult. He asked God to help him and saw lights moving around him as if ministering to him. One time, he felt as if they shook heat onto him as if from a salt shaker. He immediately felt warmed to the bone by a source warmer than gas, wood, or coal heat. On another occasion, he actually felt the covers pulled up around him and tucked in around his body.

Miraculous Events

Teachings of the Far East Masters by Baird T. Spaulding describes many miracles that have been reported in Eastern cultures for centuries. In the late 19th century, Spaulding and a team of scientists observed and later learned how to walk on water, pass through walls, and be in more than one place at a time. They observed yogis whose souls left their bodies for so long that they appeared dead and had mold and bugs on them. However, when their consciousness returned to the body, they got up and brushed themselves off as if nothing special had happened. (2)

In *Mutant Message Down Under*, Marlo Morgan described Australian Aboriginal telepathic communication, advanced healing, and other miracles that they considered commonplace. These examples demonstrate how cultural expectations about what is possible powerfully affect our perception of and participation in miracles. Aboriginal *Real People* view life as an eternal, ever-changing walk with Oneness and told Morgan, "All humans are spirits only visiting this world. All spirits are forever beings." (3)

Bernie Siegel, M.D., shared a series of miraculous events that occurred after a workshop. During a guided visualization to meet ones inner guides, he expected to see someone like Jesus or Moses. Instead, he met George—a bearded, long-haired man in a unique skullcap and robe. Some time later, he was giving a lecture but felt as if someone else was giving the talk. Afterwards, a woman from the audience said she was a medium and drew a figure she saw superimposed over Siegel. It was George. The noted psychic Olga

Worrell also described George in great detail, including his robe and old Jewish prayer cap. (4)

The book *A Promise Is a Promise* tells the miraculous story of a mother, Kaye O'Bara, who has cared for her comatose daughter Edwarda for over thirty years. Dr. Dyer states, "The most amazing part of this story concerns the effect that Edwarda has on those who have visited her. Some claim to have experienced miraculous healings, and everyone feels the unconditional love Edwarda radiates from her immobile body." For example, Anne from Venezuela had terminal brain cancer; while visiting the O'Baras, Anne prayed with Edwarda's hand on her head. Months later, medical tests showed no trace of the cancer. Mother Mary has appeared to Kaye and others many times. (5)

In 1974, I awakened in the middle of the night and saw a vision on the ceiling. A huge golden central orb had many tiny dots connected to it by golden threads. As I wondered what it all meant, a wise voice or thought said: "This is how life is. The central sphere represents God.

The infinite numbers of golden dots are like the many souls in the universe. Some of them realize Oneness and are in or on the central sphere. Some are very close but don't fully realize their inseparability from Spirit. Others believe they are quite distant from God; some of their paths are straight and simple while others appear tortuous and complicated."

The teaching continued, "The good news is that, viewed from a sufficiently enlightened perspective, the entire assemblage is seen as One. A perimeter can be drawn around even the most distant dots, revealing the unified nature of all life as love and light." This miraculous vision reminded me of my higher self and triggered an exploration of meditation, yoga, and spiritual wisdom.

An especially amazing account is the "Cokeville Miracle" as told in the book *Divine Interventions* by Dan Millman and Doug Childers. This true story occurred in 1986 in the little town of Cokeville, Wyoming. A white supremacist turned terrorist and his wife took 150 elementary school children and several teachers hostage. Armed with a shopping cart full of gasoline bombs, rifles, and handguns, they demanded ransom although his diary revealed plans to blow up the hostages, himself and his wife after receiving the money. Several hours into the siege, the bomb trigger was detonated apparently by accident and a cataclysmic explosion followed. Just after the explosion, the terrorist killed his wife, wounded a teacher, and then killed himself.

As described by Millman and Childers, "According to eyewitnesses in front of the school, bright orange fire engulfed the classroom—the whole town, by then gathered outside, watched in horror as black smoke poured out of the windows. As they rushed toward the classroom, now a burned-out shell, the ammunition stockpiled in the bottom of the cart went off in the blast, and bullets streaked through the room."

Despite all this, miraculously, only one child was hit by a stray bullet, thirty-two people received second-degree burns and no one was killed. The authors state, "But the miracle that happened in the town of Cokeville, Wyoming, wasn't fully revealed until later, when children separately began to describe to their parents, rescue workers, and police 'beings of light' who had come 'down through the ceiling.'"

Some children saw these beings as angels, others described them as being light bright light bulbs. They were warned him about the bomb and told where to safely stand.

"'I can't tell you how lucky they were,' testified bomb expert Richard Haskell of the Sweetwater County sheriff's department. 'When you look in that classroom—when you see all that charred furniture and burnt walls—it's amazing that there weren't 150 kids lying in there dead. To call it a miracle would be the understatement of the century.'" (6)

Millman and Childers also describe numerous other miracles such as sightings near Cairo, Egypt, of the "lady of light." This vision, believed to be Mary, mother of Jesus, has been seen by hundreds of thousands of persons. Numerous clear photographs of this moving, glowing figure exist with detailed testimonials by news reporters, church officials, and people of different faiths.

Another human form within a luminous cloud was seen by tens of thousands in Fatima, Portugal from 1915 to 1917. This vision, also believed to be a visitation by Mother Mary, was accompanied by a dazzling array of moving colored lights in the sky that were witnessed from miles around. The multitudes saw shiny petals fall from the sky that soon melted away. They also smelled sweet fragrances while many received miraculous healings of various injuries and illnesses.

The night before I finished my first book, *Balanced Living*, I felt a profound peace, like I had finally arrived after many years of praying, searching and working. I had originally planned to become a medical doctor (M.D.) but a series of events guided me to become a doctor of chiropractic (D.C.) That night, I deeply felt that these life changes had occurred for good reason and worked out for the best.

Early the next morning, I started to complete the last few hours of work on the manuscript. Just as I had done many times, I turned on the computer and monitor that usually showed a black screen followed by computer codes and prompts. That morning, however, the monitor *immediately* showed a vivid display of royal gold and maroon squares.

These colored squares each contained the same two letters. I rubbed my eyes and pinched myself to make sure I wasn't dreaming. The letters were D.C.! This miracle still inspires me to practice advanced chiropractic part-time and help people enjoy the many benefits of a healthy nervous system.

Conclusions and Action Steps

There are many more miracle stories out there; I've presented only a few examples. If you have been blessed with revelatory experiences, don't deny them for fear of being considered kooky. If you haven't, don't underestimate the potential for miracles in your life. As David Ben-Gurion said, "Any man who does not believe in miracles is not a realist."

Suggested action steps include:

∞ Review your life and consider if you have ever experienced a miracle—even a small one

∞ Ask your family and friends if they have ever experienced a revelation or miracle

∞ Read further about this topic

Benefit  3

A deeper understanding and peace about life's existential questions: "Who am I? Where did I come from? Why am I here? Is there a God? What happens after death?"

While sitting at the beach, I saw an elderly man walking alone. He moved slowly and periodically gazed out at the water and sky. I felt moved to talk with him and, after a few minutes of small talk, I discovered why.

As his eyes swelled with tears, he told me that his wife of forty-two years had recently died. He was especially struggling with her death because they both had lost faith in their religion many years ago. It began when they asked their minister important questions like: "Why does the church teach that an un-baptized baby might not go to heaven?" and "Why does the church teach that people who get divorced for very good reasons may not go to heaven?"

In each case, the answer was, "That's just what our church believes and you have to accept it on faith." These answers drove them away from the church and their faith. Over the years, he said, they both had come to believe that when you die, you die, and that's it.

I told him about my book *Soul Proof* and the nine categories of evidence that all people are timeless spiritual beings who, by their very nature, automatically inherit eternity. I explained that a vast amount of evidence, some of it objective and documented, strongly indicates that death is not a "good-bye" but a "see you later."

Upon hearing this information, he smiled slightly and his face lightened a bit. "I would love to believe that what you say is true," he said, "if only I had the proof. I would love to think that I will see her again, that there really is life after death."

Suddenly his eyes widened and his voice grew stronger. "There was one thing that happened that makes me think maybe I will see her again," he shared. He explained that his seventy-six year old wife had withered away to only ninety pounds after a long battle with cancer. She had lingered in a coma, curled up in the fetal position for weeks, long after doctors expected her to pass.

"Then, just 24 hours before she died," he said, "it happened." Her face became beautiful and radiant like a young woman's. She looked like she was thirty years-old again and so very peaceful. Doctors and nurses came to visit from all over the hospital. Everyone who saw her said she looked like an angel. Maybe that was God's way of letting me know that death is not the final end we thought it was."

As we said good-bye, he thanked me over and over again for telling him about all the evidence and giving him hope. I walked away with tears in my eyes, thankful for hearing yet another miracle that brings light to darkness, even though we may struggle with unanswered questions. Yes, my friend, death is only a 'see you later'—and that makes all the difference.

What about our existential questions above? Based on the collective evidence, here are the short answers:

♦ Who am I? A timeless spiritual being having a very temporary human experience—and so is everyone else

♦ Where did I come from? Another dimension, not so different or far away from ours, with a higher vibratory rate and greater awareness

♦ Why am I here? To love, learn, experience, serve, and enjoy

♦ Is there a God? Yes. We'll discuss the nature of All That Is later

♦ What happens after death? We continue to live at the level of love and consciousness we had when we changed worlds. The quality of our experience can change anytime we do

Since all life is miraculous and connected, the highest path is to treat *all* people with love and reverence. Perhaps this compiled evidence of our spiritual natures will help us focus more on our essential oneness instead of our relatively minor differences. Hopefully, humanity is evolving to the point where dissimilarities—whether in race, religion, ethnicity, gender, age, sexual orientation, philosophy, outward appearance, and special challenges—are appreciated instead of feared.

It seems to me that a stronger knowledge of our spiritual heritage would naturally lead to more tolerance and respect. Greater identification with our timeless natures should reprioritize our lives so that wealth, power, and possessions take their rightful secondary status. Establishing and maintaining peace and justice—not war and inequities—will surely be of paramount importance as we increasingly remember our interconnectedness.

The elderly man at the beach felt renewed hope when he saw just a glimpse of hope. In the same way, even a basic understanding of the questions above can lighten your load and brighten your day.

Evidence Category 4

Scientific Input

Late into the night, a scientist works alone in his laboratory. Suddenly, he hears a voice that explains how to perfect his invention. When the inventor asks the voice to identify itself, he is told it's a spirit visiting from the "second millennium." The scientist uses the information to successfully complete details on a machine that nearly everyone has used and benefited from.

Physicist Chester Carlson, inventor of the Xerox machine, received key ideas in his laboratory when he heard voices that explained the principles of making copies. *Science* magazine reported that Carlson left millions in his will to psychical research because, 'He felt that science should try to reach into the mystery of survival after death.'" Renowned reincarnation researcher Ian Stevenson, M.D., is one such beneficiary of Carlson's donations.

In this section, I'll present evidence for our spiritual natures from a scientific perspective. Webster's primary definition of 'science' is: "possession of knowledge as distinguished from ignorance or misunderstanding; accumulated and accepted knowledge that has been systematized and formulated with reference to the discovery of general truths." (1) There is a wealth of diverse scientific evidence that strongly supports the existence of a spiritual reality.

The nature of this subject does not easily lend itself to double blind studies although some serious research has begun. As such, I will cite scientific findings and quote numerous scientists. Some of this information may be complex to the reader, but the knowledge gained is well worth the effort.

Categories discussed include: history of scientific investigations, views by eminent scientists, input from physical sciences, the nature of reality, the relative reality of time, and humans as beings of energy and consciousness.

History of Scientific Investigations

Since the 19ᵗʰ century, many respected scientists have investigated and demonstrated the existence of unseen realities. Societies for psychical research were formed in the U.S., England, and France. Some of the best minds of that era were involved, for example, Drs. William James, Frederick Myers, and J.B. Rhine.

After many years of investigating the validity of communicating with those who had passed on, world renowned scientist Sir Oliver Lodge concluded, "Basing my conclusions on experience, I am absolutely convinced not only of survival but of demonstrated survival, demonstrated by occasional interaction with matter in such a way as to produce physical results."

Sir William Crookes, a prominent physicist and chemist, invented the Crooke's tube and radiometer and discovered the element thallium. He and his observers investigated two of England's greatest mediums using strict scientific controls and could not expose either one. To the contrary, he found these phenomena to be incredible evidence of life after death and concluded, "Outside our scientific knowledge there exists a Force exercised by intelligence differing from the ordinary intelligence common to mortals." (2)

There are numerous published experimental and case studies exploring survival after death. In addition, supporting *empirical evidence*, which is based on direct personal experience, is as strong as that of any science. However, spiritually based topics are often held to an unjustly higher standard of proof.

Abuse of power by the established church, for example, condemning eminent scientists like Galileo and Copernicus, contributed to science's avoidance of spiritually related subjects. Science is just now recovering from this over-reaction against the influence of the church. Even today, however, some academicians are censored or punished for pursuing interests in topics involving consciousness or other spiritual themes.

In *Natural Grace*, respected scientist Rupert Sheldrake says: "The soul is the animating principle, that which makes living things alive. . . A lot of the present confusion began in the philosophy of Rene Descartes in the seventeenth century. Descartes said that the whole of Nature is a machine; it is inanimate. In effect, he withdrew the soul from Nature, from all animals and plants, and from the human body as well. Before that, the soul was believed to permeate the whole body." Sheldrake says we can go beyond Cartesian dualism by recognizing the existence of fields in magnets, gravity, quantum matter, and biology. Likewise, he concludes, the soul can be understood as a field of energy or consciousness. (3)

In my radio interview with Jeffrey Mishlove, Ph.D., author of *The Roots of Consciousness*, he stated:

> We live in a very unusual age. The modern Western world is almost unique in all of world history in terms of its denial of the spiritual, the paranormal side of life. Ancient myths about the origin of the universe posit that in the beginning was spirit, in the beginning was God, this Oneness. Oneness was conscious and, for a variety of reasons in different myths, desired to create a universe. The sense is that energy, matter, time, and space all evolved out of consciousness.
>
> Today, the conventional scientific view is that consciousness is sort of a product of the brain but there are some very serious problems with that position. This view, known technically as *epiphenomenalism*, is that somehow consciousness emerges from something that is not conscious, that is purely physical. It doesn't satisfy anyone, philosophically speaking.
>
> Although it is the popular view among modern academics, it is seriously flawed. We now have leading edge biologists, physicists, and neurophysiologists saying maybe consciousness is something elemental. Maybe it's just as fundamental as space and time or maybe it's even more fundamental. (4)

Views of Eminent Scientists

Dr. Friedbert Karger, German physicist at Munich's Max Planck Institute, has extensively studied afterlife phenomena and states: "The consciousness—or soul—of a man lives beyond the body. The body is a tool that consciousness uses. When the body dies, the soul remains. . . Death is not an end but a transition from one state to another." He says that many famous physicists have expressed an interest in the spiritual world. (5)

Max Planck, founder of quantum physics, said "Spirit is the original basis of all matter, reality, true existence." Albert Einstein stated, "Everyone who is seriously involved in the pursuit of science becomes convinced that a Spirit is manifest in the Laws of the Universe." Thomas Edison believed in life beyond death and apparently visited beatific realms just before death. After momentarily awakening from a coma, he stated: "It is very beautiful over there."

Wilder Penfield, M.D., is widely considered to be the father of neurosurgery and is responsible for much of our current understanding of brain function. Like some of his medical colleagues, Penfield thought for many years that there was no consciousness independent of the brain. He believed that all human behavior could be explained on the basis of brain function. After *fifty years of research*, he changed his mind.

As Penfield said in his last book, *The Mystery of the Mind*, "I came to take seriously, even to believe, that the consciousness of man, the mind, is NOT something to be reduced to brain mechanism. . . What a thrill it is, then, to discover that the scientist, too, can legitimately believe in the existence of the spirit! Possibly the scientist and the physician could add something by stepping outside the laboratory and the consulting room to reconsider these strangely gifted human beings about us. Where did the mind—call it the spirit if you like—come from? Who can say? It exists." (6)

The delightful movie *"What the Bleep Do We Know?"* contains numerous quotes by esteemed physicists and physicians who believe that both science and spirituality are necessary to fully understand the magnitude and mystery of life. The website (www. whatthebleep.com) contains many quotes by well known scientists including this one by Stephen W. Hawking: "To confine our attention to terrestrial matters would be to limit the human spirit."

In *Changes of Mind*, New York State University researcher Jenny Wade, Ph.D., states, "Discoveries in the physical sciences—notably quantum physics, field and chaos theory, and holography—are introducing a new concept of reality more congruent with the Eastern and ancient mystical worldviews. The new paradigm differs from Newtonianism on the fundamentals, such as time and space, matter and mind, and science and spirituality." Of this new paradigm, Nobel Laureate George Wald, Ph.D., states the assumption that mind ". . . has existed always as the matrix, the source and condition of physical reality—that the stuff of which physical reality is composed is mind-stuff." (7)

True science seeks to explain and understand without rejecting the unknown out-of-hand. Says noted psychiatrist Brian Weiss, M.D., "Being analytical is completely compatible with being open-minded... science and spirituality, long considered antithetical, are coming together. Physicists and psychiatrists are becoming the mystics of the modern time. We are confirming what prior mystics knew intuitively. We are all divine beings." (8)

In a similar vein, Melvin Morse, M.D., esteemed pediatric NDE researcher and author, adds: "It is scientifically respectable to argue that consciousness survives death. . . . My research has shown that not only are near-death experiences real, but that by studying the mechanism of the experiences, we learn that all human beings are interconnected with the universe and everything in it that ever was and ever shall be." (9)

May I suggest that readers take a few slow deep breaths here so they can wrap their minds around what is being said by so many eminent scientists: Spirit exists; we are all Divine beings; we're all interconnected; physical reality is composed of mind-stuff. The synthesis of science and spirituality has created a paradigm shift with immense personal and planetary implications.

Willis Harmon, Ph.D., emeritus professor at Stanford and founder of the Institute of Noetic Sciences, stated in his book *Global Mind Change*: "There is a tremendous amount of empirical, anecdotal, clinical, and traditional evidence suggesting that in some sense the essence of the person survives physical death, and that the realm of the after-death is not so discontinuous with earthly life as we might have been led to assume . . . death appears less as an extinction than as an awakening to `where one was all along'. At death, the center of awareness shifts from the physical to higher planes (with perhaps a period of confusion and/or sleepy resting in between). We don't go somewhere at death; we are already there. As this new view becomes real in our lives, fear of death disappears. We couldn't nonexist if we wanted to." (10)

Impressive scientific research has been performed at the University of Arizona by Gary Schwartz, Ph.D. and his team. Dr.

Schwartz, a former professor at Harvard and Yale, has had over four hundred scientific papers published in peer-reviewed scientific journals, presented over six hundred papers at scientific meetings, edited eleven academic books, and co-authored, with Linda Russek, Ph.D., *The Living Energy Universe*.

As described in *The Afterlife Experiments: Breakthrough Scientific Evidence Of Life After Death*, Schwartz investigated five mediums and their abilities to truly communicate with souls of departed people. Using strict laboratory procedures, the 'readers' or mediums could not see or hear the 'sitters' or subjects. Further, he states, "The medium had no way of knowing anything about the sitter—not the name, not even the sex, age bracket, background, city of residence, or any other details."

Of the findings, Dr. Schwartz comments: "Scientists and nonscientists alike are experiencing a test of faith—in this case, whether we can put our belief in the scientific method itself. Because if we are to put our faith in the scientific method, and trust what the data reveal, we are led to the hypothesis that the universe is more wondrous than imagined in our wildest flights of fancy. . . . the totality of the findings are surprisingly consistent with the concept of life after death and what we call the 'living soul hypothesis' . . ." (11)

Since his work is discussed more fully in the "Reincarnation Evidence" chapter, I will only briefly mention here the painstaking research by Ian Stevenson, M.D. Regarding factors that shape who and how we are, he states: "I do not propose reincarnation as a substitute for present or future knowledge of genetics and environmental influences. I think of it as a third factor contributing to the formation of human personality and of some physical features and abnormalities. I am, however, convinced that it deserves attention for the additional explanatory value that it has for numerous unsolved problems of psychology and medicine." (12)

Finally, although he is not a scientist, I mention attorney Sidney L. Freeman's research in this section because of his methodical investigation of diverse evidence. His book *Life After Death: A Survey of the Cumulative Evidence* was a great assistance to my research. Mr. Freeman states, "One of the greatest mysteries facing us all is what happens to us when we die. Is death the end of everything? Or is there something beyond death? If so, exactly what is it? . . . I set out to prove it—one way or the other. I went about it like a lawyer—to see what the evidence showed. Did the evidence prove life after death to be a scientific fact or was it pure fiction?"

Freeman recognized the difficulties inherent in scientifically proving matters of spirit and stated, "The fact is that the unexplainable phenomena which have been so puzzling to our scientists do not have their origin in *our science*. . . Even under our laws of science, 'not proven' is not always the equivalent of 'not true.' This has been demonstrated time and time again."

After examining much evidence and many firsthand reports, Freeman's reply to the question "Can life after death be scientifically proven?" was: "Yes, it has been—to a number of those who seriously delved into it, including some of the world's greatest scientists, as well as many prominent physicians, psychiatrists, psychologists, professors, businessmen, statesmen, lawyers, clergymen and major Church organizations. . . . I have concluded, *from the evidence*, that life after death is a scientific fact. All of us, without exception, will find ourselves in another, strange and intriguing new world when our physical body expires." (13)

Input from Physical Sciences

When asked to describe the nature of reality, quantum physicists describe solid matter as intermittently having properties of energy or light waves. Conversely, energy or light waves sometimes have properties of solid matter. Perhaps the most accurate description of the nature of reality is, then, neither that of solid mass nor pure energy, but more an interplay or flow between the two. Great spiritual teachers have long taught that God is Light and that this phenomenon permeates all existence. Now scientists similarly describe life as a mysterious interplay between matter, energy, and light.

Einstein proposed the theory of relativity: e = m(c squared); that is, energy equals mass multiplied by the speed of light squared. In other words, *energy and mass are transmutable and interchangeable* under certain conditions. Energy and mass are not static, separate entities but, rather, dynamic, intermingling phenomena that overlap in all life.

David Deutsch, Ph.D., one of the world's leading theoretical physicists, recently proposed the existence of parallel universes. By applying the laws of quantum physics, generally considered applicable only on the subatomic level, Dr. Deutsch argues that we each simultaneously live in innumerable parallel existences or states of being. We live not in a single universe, he says, but in a vast and rich multiverse in which other versions of ourselves live out other options we've encountered.

Even after someone dies, other copies of him or her might remain alive in other realities. Says Deutsch, "The primary purpose of science is to understand what the world is like. Everything else that science does—test theories, produce new technologies—is incidental to this fundamental purpose of gaining a deeper understanding of reality." (14)

Chemical sciences also support the complex and *ephemeral nature* of existence. All 'solid' objects consist primarily of space with tiny atoms whirring at high speeds within the void. When you rest your hand on a table, the atoms that make up your hand and the table interchange. The most exciting implication of this is there is *no meaningful separation* in the unity of life.

Dr. Melvin Morse asked leading theoretical physicists about the nature of reality. Their best current understanding is described by the term 'non-local' reality in which time and space do not exist, and everything happens at once. One child who survived a near-death experience called it "the really real" place.

Morse comments: "On the one hand, we have theoretical physicists who have been trying to explain to us for the past fifty years that our material world is actually based on pulsating, endless patterns of light and energy. On the other hand, we have mystics, psychics, and those who have had near-death experiences telling us that they have had a glimpse of a level of reality in which all knowledge is contained, time and space are meaningless, and is filled with a loving light." (15)

Esteemed physicist David Bohm describes the ultimate nature of reality as unified energy that undergoes constant change. In his view, life is fundamentally best described as an enormous totality of energy in perpetual motion. Our physical world is like a tiny ripple on a vast sea, a wavelike excitation on top of this seething energy soup. Just as each fragment of a hologram contains information about the entire image, each human being in some sense contains the essence of the universe.

Dr. Bohm postulates two levels of reality that coexist and overlap. The *material order* is the manifestation of energy which is perceived by our brains as physical reality bound by time and space. The *absolute or implicate order* is infinite, consists of pure energy, and transcends physicality. Together, these two orders comprise an undivided whole that constantly flows and changes.

Even "empty space" is full of this energy that ultimately merges and unites in a *holomovement*, Bohm's term for the dynamic and holographic nature of reality. Western philosophers such as Plato, Plotinus, Spinoza, and Hegel have described this deep unitive reality for centuries, as have physicists for over 50 years.

In his book, *The Medium, the Mystic, and the Physicist*, Lawrence LeShan states, "It is very difficult for the modern scientist to think about the possibility of the personality surviving biological death because of his assumption that brain and mind are the same. This is accepted as the 'truth,' and it is rarely realized that this is an assumption and that other conceptualizations are possible. For example, there is the viewpoint taken by Bergson, James, Eccles, Burt, and others which is perhaps best summed up in the words of Sir Charles Sherrington: 'Mental phenomena on examination do not seem amenable to understanding under physics and chemistry. I have therefore to think of the brain as an organ of liaison between energy and mind, but not as a converter of energy into mind or vice versa.'" (16)

The Nature of Reality

It's a scientific fact that the human brain and accompanying five senses, amazing as they may be, are nevertheless limited in perceiving reality. For example, humans can't hear a dog whistle, or differentiate between eight shades of white like hummingbirds can. What appears to our eyes as white light is really, as revealed by a simple prism, a rainbow of colors. The electro-magnetic spectrum contains many wavelengths, x-rays for example, that human senses can not detect.

Here's another scientific fact that highlights the brain's limited perceptual ability that contributes to humanity's collective delusion. Even though we appear to be standing still, the earth travels at 66,000 miles per hour and completes a trip of 595,000,000 miles around the sun every year. At the same time, our planet rotates around its own axis. Why should we rely solely on our five senses for an accurate understanding of reality when we can't even detect all this commotion?

Acclaimed inventor and mathematician Buckminster Fuller stated that 99% of reality is intangible to our senses. Important phenomena like air, electricity and gravity are real yet escape detection by conventional human senses. The "nonsensate world", that great majority of reality that cannot be experienced by our senses, is nonetheless just as real. The point? There's more to life than meets the eye and other sense organs. If we believe only what our senses tell us, we are missing out on much of reality.

States Deepak Chopra, M.D.,

Sight, hearing, touch, taste, and smell serve to reinforce the same message: Things are what they seem. According to this reality, the earth is flat, the ground beneath your feet is stationary, the sun rises in the east and sets in the west, all because it seems that way to the senses. . . (The truth is) I am not my atoms, they come and go. I am not my thoughts, they come and go. I am not my ego, my self-image changes. I am above and beyond these: I am the witness, the interpreter, the Self beyond the self-image. This Self is ageless and timeless. . .

Although our package of skin and bones looks very convincing, it is a mask, an illusion, disguising our true self, which has no limitations. . . . We are not the body. We are not the mind. We are the ones who have mind and body. . . There is no higher purpose than trying to open your awareness until you can consciously experience the full impact of this reality in all its truth, wonder, and sacredness. (17)

In *Doors of Perception*, Aldous Huxley compared the human brain to a powerful receiver that is capable of picking up many more and distant signals than it usually does. For example, light and sound waves are transmitted through time and space indefinitely. We couldn't function without sensory selectivity so 90% of the brain's function is inhibitory, that is, filters incoming information. The brain limits sensory input so we can discern only that information necessary for optimal functioning. This dampening was necessary for human survival in the past but at this stage in human evolution, it is more adaptive to perceive reality on a grander scale.

The transition between ice, water, and steam provides a useful model for better understanding the nature of reality. These potential forms of H2O mirror our alternating perceptions from a seemingly solid human being to an invisible being of energy. Ice and steam are merely alternate forms of water under different environmental conditions. Likewise, formed physicality and formless consciousness are merely varying reflections of the Life Force.

This water model conveys other useful parallels for better understanding physical and spiritual dimensions. Molecules in ice vibrate more slowly than those in steam. Similarly, we are told, physical dimensions have a slower vibrational frequency than more etheric ones.

Finally, water demonstrates properties of apparent separateness (dualism) while simultaneously being unified with all water. For example, a glass of water appears to be a separate, distinct object. Let the water evaporate or pour it into the ocean, however, and it becomes part of the greater whole. It rejoins the cycle of water, evaporation and condensation. We each, as souls, are like that. Various spiritual teachings compare human souls to drops of water whereas God is like the ocean. As the ice/water/steam model indicates, there is no clear demarcation between where one ends and the other begins.

In *The Varieties of Religious Experience*, Dr. William James, one of America's preeminent behavioral scientists, stated: ". . . our normal waking consciousness, rational consciousness as we call it, is but one special type of consciousness, whilst all about it, parted from it by the filmiest of screens, there lie potential forms of consciousness entirely different. . . . No account of the universe in its totality can be final which leaves these other forms of consciousness quite disregarded." (18)

Various sources of Native spirituality have taught that God is like a master potter or painter that creates different vessels or paintings and then sets them aside to create yet new works. Similarly, Hindu models view the Supreme as variously inhaling—resulting in a formless creation—then exhaling with formed aspects of reality manifesting. These ancient teachings are particularly impressive when compared with quantum physics' view of the alternating wave/particle nature of energy/matter which results in an apparent formless/formed continuum.

The Relative Reality of Time

Time's illusory nature is a difficult concept to grasp but realizing the *relative reality* of time is a start. Eternity is perhaps best depicted as being comprised of a series of *eternal now* moments. From a human perspective, time is real and useful for functioning in the world. However, from a spiritual perspective, the past and future are illusory; all we have is now. Or, more accurately—but harder to conceptualize—there is no such thing as time. All life is one endless dance of energy as the Ground of All Being unceasingly manifests itself with infinite possibilities. We are timeless beings of energy.

Peter Russell, DCS, author of *Waking Up in Time*, was a protégé of Stephen Hawking at the University of Cambridge and is one of the world's foremost mathematicians and physicists. He says that time, space, and matter are only relatively real; only light can be considered absolutely real irrespective of surrounding conditions. Light and consciousness, he notes, have important parallels with much more than just semantic similarities. Russell defines consciousness as the ability to have experiences; it is like a screen that the movie projector needs for the movie to be experienced.

Science, Russell says, may soon be forced to accept that consciousness is primary just as Eastern philosophies have long taught. The Christian mystic Meister Eckhart was attacked for his statements that he was part of and one with God but now science is pointing to the inseparability of consciousness. Dr. Russell encourages meditative and centering practices for a firsthand experience of time's relative reality. (19)

Earth's indigenous cultures viewed time as a circular or cyclical, rather than linear, phenomenon. The symbol for infinity is a horizontal figure eight that has no beginning and no end. One indication that time isn't really real is the fluctuating nature of time. Consider how long an hour seems while waiting in a traffic jam versus watching an exciting movie. Notice how the journey toward a destination seems to take longer than the trip back home. Older persons often report an accelerated perception of time as they age.

Realizing that time is illusory sets the stage for understanding life's apparent injustices and tragedies. From a purely physical perspective that emphasizes time, the death of a five-year-old is a great and senseless tragedy. Only from a timeless soul-perspective does it seem less so although some grieving understandably remains.

Spiritual regression is similar to past life regression only involves longer sessions under deeper hypnosis. Subjects, who recall time in spiritual dimensions in between physical lifetimes, describe time in a unique way. Their soul group interactions on the other side are like an eternal poker game and periodically a soul says: `Don't deal me in this hand; I'm leaving for a physical incarnation. I'll see you all shortly.' Many years in earth time then pass, but this seems like just a few minutes in spirit world. Soon the soul returns and says: `OK, I'm back. Deal me in.'

If this discussion of the relative reality of time is difficult for you to comprehend, consider this ancient Hindu metaphor about eternity. The Himalayas are an immense range of granite mountains. Imagine that a dove with a silk scarf in its beak flies over the mountains every one thousand years and lightly brushes the peaks with the scarf. Consider how long it would take for this process to erode these majestic mountains completely flat—that's the first day of never-ending eternity.

Humans as Beings of Energy and Consciousness

Humans are beings of energy who appear to be solid matter, an illusion that makes it difficult to accurately apprehend reality. Science has long proven that 'solid matter' is largely space and energy but most people haven't realized the implications of this finding. For example, if a hydrogen atom's nucleus were the size of a marble, its single electron would be a quarter mile away! This model helps us fathom that we are comprised of solid matter but, rather, energy, light, and space.

An electromagnetic field operates within and around all life; humans are *bio-energetic beings*. This life force is even in rocks and other apparently inert forms since all matter is a manifestation of energy. As Russian researchers of Kirlian photography have stated, "All living things—plants, animals, and humans not only have a physical body made of atoms and molecules but also a counterpart body of energy" which they termed the 'biological plasma body.'

The human heart produces electromagnetic frequencies that are 100 to 1000 times larger than brain waves. Elmer Green, Ph.D., longtime biofeedback researcher at the Menninger Clinic, says these electrical waves from the heart can be measured four to five feet away from the body. Thus, the body's sixty trillion cells are influenced by the heart's electric field every time it beats. A greater realization of our energetic nature is life-changing to say the least. As Robert O. Becker, M.D., author of *The Body Electric*, states: "A knowledge of life's electrical dimension has yielded fundamental insights into pain, healing, growth, consciousness, the nature of life itself . . ." [20]

The science of chiropractic health care has a strongly spiritual philosophical foundation that dates to the nineteenth century. The founders of chiropractic proposed that reality ultimately consists of *Universal Intelligence* that made and sustains the universe and all life. A portion of this life-force, termed 'Innate Intelligence', resides within all creation. Their vision for chiropractic was to help connect 'man the physical with man the spiritual.' Healing, they said, occurs, 'above-down, inside-out' when there are no interferences to the optimal flow of intelligence and energy.

Chinese philosophies have long viewed humans as having an electrical component to their total makeup. In this model, humans are beings of energy with a flow of bipolar electromagnetic power that runs and heals the body. This mysterious force, chi, is variously termed *ki* in Japan, *prana* in India, and *vital force* in the Western world. Some sensitive persons can see or otherwise sense the aura or energy field of others, another indication of its reality.

The First Law of Thermodynamics, the Law of the Conservation of Energy, states that energy cannot be destroyed but merely changes form. Things may change from one form to another but that is not the end of them. For example, the *potential energy* in a piece of wood changes to *thermal energy* when it is burned. Ashes remain as freed heat energy radiates in all directions, but the essence of the wood—energy—is not destroyed.

The collective evidence indicates that the same law applies to humans who, despite their physical disguises, are really beings of energy.

Conclusions and Action Steps

As you have seen, there is significant scientific evidence that no one really dies. This is especially important for skeptics who value objective scientific proof. Further research on afterlife and spiritual topics is needed. Drs. Gary Schwartz, Joseph B. Rhine, Ian Stevenson, Gertrude Schmeidler, and other behavioral scientists have already contributed serious, scientifically acceptable studies in this field. This scientific proof can help us enjoy life without fear and know that 'the really real place' awaits us all.

Suggested action steps:

- ∞ Discuss these issues with family and friends; how does this information fit with your religious and philosophical beliefs?

- ∞ Join a study group or book club that considers these topics in greater depth

- ∞ Read further and explore the vast amount of scientific evidence for yourself

- ∞ Take physics and chemistry courses so you better understand the scientific principles discussed in this section

Benefit ∞ 4

Increased clarity and courage to follow your purpose and heartfelt joys

"How can I know what my soul's missions are?" is a very important question since, as we just discussed, much scientific evidence indicates we are spiritual beings.

"Margaret", an older female in North Carolina, told my workshop group that she didn't know what her mission was. "I've tried and tried to figure it out" she stated, "and I can't come up with anything." In an attempt to help clarify her life purposes, I asked how she spent her time. "Over the last seven years, I've helped eight friends and family members who were very ill and stayed with them until they passed on. I've been so busy that I don't have time to figure out my soul's missions."

If only all questions were so easy to solve.

Realizing our greatness as infinite souls bestows many gifts. One is trusting yourself enough to follow your greatest joys. What clearer way could Creator reveal your unique path than by what most excites and interests you? As Joseph Campbell said: "If you follow your bliss, you put yourself on a kind of track that has been there the whole while, waiting for you, and the life you ought to be living is the one you are living."

Follow your heart, do what you feel called to do. Trust your intuition, that wise inner voice that guides you toward your mission in life. The pieces of life's puzzle will fall in place as more and more persons—starting with you—pursue their bliss. Our souls came to earth to learn and teach lessons, love and serve one another, and enjoy life.

Our souls, in alignment with God's plan to varying degrees, chose missions before they came to earth. Those missions are our dreams, visions, and greatest desires. Everyone has a life-vision and special talents they were meant to share. Universe totally supports those who assist God's plan to bring peace, joy, love and light on earth.

This is not just lofty, impractical spiritual advice; it's useful information that can increase the quality and quantity of life. For example, the most common time for heart attacks is early Monday morning. Day after day, year after year of following a path with no heart or soul literally compromises ones anatomical heart.

I've counseled a number of persons who hated their work but were afraid to follow their bliss. "After I retire, then I'll start that little business I've always dreamed of" they say. When I ask about their life's dream, they invariably pause for a moment. Then their eyes light up as they describe what they would do "*if* only. . ." The truth is, each person *can* follow their calling. Doing so, at least part time, is a key to experiencing heaven on earth.

Attending to the soul's mission is usually a multi-dimensional process. We each have numerous roles in life—family member, significant other, friend, worker, church member, community participant, and individual. Following your bliss doesn't mean forsaking all other roles and just focusing on one aspect. On the contrary, being totally successful and achieving our soul's mission means meeting all our roles impeccably.

Fulfilling our various roles can be challenging, but it's possible. Making a commitment to identify and pursue your dreams is a first step. Some people have the circumstances and chutzpah to make abrupt changes and follow their bliss full time. Others may choose to make a more gradual transition over time. Whichever path you choose, start *now*!

Let your heart and soul dream for a moment using your fullest imagination and passion: if you knew you could not fail, what would you do? Let the images flow and feel the excitement as, perhaps for the first time, you become aware of your soul's calling. Following it puts us in touch with the joy and peace that is our birthright.

At the same time, be wise about it. A Middle Eastern saying for this is: 'Trust Allah, but tie up your camel.' Daily living requires a certain income to survive so don't rush off and quit your day job prematurely. I know some people who did and wish they hadn't. Stay with your current work and expand your services until you *grow into* your higher calling.

To begin identifying your soul's calling, close your eyes, let yourself become relaxed, and ask for assistance from God and the heavenly host. Give thanks for guidance and clarity in realizing your soul's mission. Then listen quietly for that still small voice within. Now answer the following questions by noting the very first response that spontaneously arises. Note any clues that arise spontaneously such as words, pictures, feelings, colors or other persons and places.

◆ What are you naturally good at?

◆ What would you do if money were no object?

◆ What would you do if you had only one year to live?

◆ What would you do if you knew you couldn't fail?

◆ What would you do without pay because you enjoy it?

◆ What do you read and talk about in your spare time?

◆ What chokes you up, gives you goose bumps, cold chills, and tears in your eyes or pressure over your chest?

◆ How do you feel called to assist the emergence of heaven on earth?

Some people think that their souls' calling has to be a world changing outreach. The old church hymn, "Brighten the corner where you are" lends a hint. Do the best you can within your sphere of influence and know that's enough. Let your compassionate heart show you who needs help and how. And don't forget to put yourself on your list of priorities.

Someday we each will fly away from this demanding but wonderfully instructive classroom. Until then, our task is to learn, love, serve, enjoy, and leave this planet a better place than when we arrived. Why not do it with style and grace as powerful, totally successful humans who clearly remember they are spiritual beings!

Evidence Category 5

Paranormal Input

Despite a $25,000 prize—a king's ransom in 1927—no one had successfully flown solo across the Atlantic. How did the winner do it? He said 'ghostly presences' guided him and took over when he succumbed to fatigue and sleep. The pilot described these phantoms as transparent, moving, speaking with human voices, and friendly. These 'emissaries from a spirit world' were, said the flier, like a gathering of family and friends he had known before. Colonel Charles A. Lindbergh wrote about this spirit-assisted flight in his autobiography *The Spirit of St. Louis.*

Lindbergh's experience could be categorized as paranormal. Webster defines *paranormal* as: "Beyond the range of scientifically known or recognizable phenomena; rare; supernatural."

However, as C.W. Leadbeater stated, "It is one of the commonest of mistakes to consider that the limit of our power of perception is also the limit of all there is to perceive." Just because something can not currently be fully explained by scientific method doesn't preclude its existence.

In this section, I'll discuss input from authentic mediums and channelers and other paranormal sources. Many people aren't aware of the legitimacy of this category because past references to the paranormal were sometimes linked with the occult, satanic, weird, or nonsensical. Examining these topics with open-minded skepticism, however, may fill in pieces of life's puzzle for you.

Some churches and people dismiss mediumship as demonic in nature. However, history reports multiple examples of people and miracles that were considered as demonic by the established church and now are viewed as valid. For example, the apparitions at Lourdes, France are now considered as blessed, but in the 19ᵗʰ century, Bernadette Soubirous—an ignorant peasant girl who communicated with Mother Mary—was considered mentally incompetent. Authentic mediums categorically deny any evil intention but, rather, consider their special gifts as a sacred trust to be used to help others.

Admittedly, there are and have been fraudulent mediums and channelers and caution must be exercised as with any endeavor. Capricious or malicious spirits also appear to exist; just because a discarnate being can communicate with our dimension doesn't mean it is wise and trustworthy. As such, mediums must use discernment in evaluating the message and the messenger.

If just one medium, however, has genuine abilities to communicate with spirit world, then that information is vital. There are a number of mediums whose work has been authenticated by top scientists and many clients. As you will see, their messages are overwhelmingly reassuring that there is life after death for everyone. Being with the Infinite Light, these mediums agree, is always an open-ended possibility because that's our Source and birthright.

Historical Perspectives

In a 1981 Gallup poll, 42% claimed to have had some type of contact with the dead but this is not just a recent phenomena. Reports of communication with discarnate beings—souls without bodies—date back thousands of years. In more modern times, the scientific study of spirit contact began when the Society for Psychical Research was founded in London in 1882.

Many respected scientists and well-known persons have believed in the existence of spiritual dimensions. Sir Isaac Newton deemed the subject of psychic phenomena worthy of research but was censured by the church and peers. Sigmund Freud was a member of the English and American Societies for Psychical Research and stated, "If I had my life to live over again, I should devote myself to psychical research rather than to psychoanalysis." Carl Jung also researched and wrote extensively about the paranormal. J.B. Rhine, professor of psychology at Duke University, primarily focused on ESP research but before his death in 1980, he called for "further experimentation to learn about death and postmortem survival."

In *We Don't Die*, Martin and Romanowski state that other highly respected figures, from Socrates and Plato to Edgar Cayce and Helen Keller had personal experiences in contacting departed souls. Séances occurred in the Lincoln White House. In an interview with *Scientific American*, Thomas Edison stated, "Therefore, if personality exists after what we call death, it's reasonable to conclude that those who leave this earth would like to communicate with those they have left here. . . . I do claim that it is possible to construct an apparatus which will be so delicate that if there are personalities in another existence or sphere who wish to get in touch with us . . . this apparatus will at least give them a better opportunity." Edison was working on a machine to communicate with spirits but passed on before it was completed. [1]

Brian Weiss, M.D., notes, "As I have explored more and more of the human mind and the limits of consciousness, I have come across some people with extraordinary abilities. Some can access information not normally available though the five senses. They seem to possess a sixth sense, an inner knowing or intuition, and sometimes the information received in this manner can be quite accurate. Others have mediumistic abilities, the capacity to receive and to transmit messages and knowledge from beings on 'the other side,' or from other sources of consciousness outside the usual limits of the body and the brain." [2]

Authentic Mediums

The five mediums I will quote are considered valid and authentic by trusted experts in the fields of psychiatry and psychology. John Edward was endorsed by Raymond Moody, M.D., Ph.D. and Gary Schwartz, Ph.D. Sylvia Browne received endorsements from Caroline Myss, Ph.D., and Melvin Morse, M.D. George Anderson is considered to be a valid medium by Brian Weiss, M.D. and Dr. Schwartz. James Van Praagh was also investigated and verified by Dr. Weiss. Rosemary Altea is endorsed by Drs. Bernie Siegel and Brian Weiss. More importantly, the authenticity of these mediums has been proven by many satisfied clients from a wide variety of backgrounds.

In his book *The Afterlife Experiments*, Gary Schwartz, Ph.D., reviews his research on mediums and concludes, "In the experiments, information was consistently retrieved that can best be explained as coming from living souls. . . . information was obtained before the medium ever spoke with the sitters (subjects). Information sometimes comes that the sitter disagrees with but that turns out to be correct. Also, mediums are sometimes corrected by deceased people. The data appears to be as valid, convincing, and living as the mediums, sitters, skeptics, and scientists themselves. That's what the experimental data unmistakably shows." (3)

He believes that many who call themselves mediums are relying on "cold reading" techniques as skeptics have correctly asserted. In his experiments, however, every conceivable measure was used to ensure valid readings. Magicians, other scientists, and professional documentarians with videotapes assisted to spot any cheating. Schwartz says that no one who observed their work and data has been able to point out any flaws in the scientific methodology or produce any rational alternate explanations for the findings. Statistical analyses show that the chances their results could have occurred randomly are less than 1 in one trillion. Finding a probability of chance in the 1 out of 100 or 1000 range is the usual requirement for publishing research in respected journals.

That we can communicate with spirit beings makes perfect sense to me. As Sylvia Browne states, "Almost every religion on earth accepts the fact that our spirits survive death. But tell people you can communicate with those spirits and they will think you are nuts. So spirits exist, but we can't communicate with them? I think *that's* nuts. Of course we can!" (4)

That discernment by authentic mediums is not mind reading, or telepathy, is evidenced in several ways. First, mediums report communications from the souls who come through, not necessarily those whom subjects hope to contact. Recorded accounts of actual sessions show validated mediums insisting on a given point, even when the subject denies it. Occasionally, messages reveal future events that subjects could not be thinking of since they haven't happened. Finally, some readings contain information from the past that subjects definitely did not know.

In *We Are Not Forgotten*, Martin and Romanowski give an example of this latter point. While doing a reading for a female client, George Anderson shared that her deceased uncle was profusely apologizing for his behavior while on earth and was ashamed of himself. The woman vehemently replied that her uncle had nothing to apologize for; he was a pillar of their church and community and a great person. George didn't retreat from his earlier statements and continued describing how upset the uncle was about what he did to his family. The woman reiterated that there must be some mistake because her uncle was a fabulous person who had very good relationships with the entire family. The rest of the reading was accurate and, as she left, the woman said she would play the taped session for her family.

Two years later, the same woman returned to George for a second reading. He sees thousands of clients each year and can't recall details of the many readings he's performed over the years. As the reading began, George quickly described the uncle coming through again and apologizing profusely. This time, the woman reacted very differently: "'You're g--damned right he should apologize! That son of a bitch! I'd like to go to the cemetery, dig him up, and rip him to pieces!'" the woman exclaimed angrily. George was startled. Obviously he'd hit a nerve, but he continued, listening carefully and then repeating what he'd psychically heard. 'Your uncle is confessing that he molested his nephew. . . He says he was sexually molesting your brother.'"

The woman confirmed this information and shared that she had played the taped first session for family members. When her now middle-aged brother heard the tape, he burst into tears and told them he has been molested by that uncle but was too afraid and ashamed to tell anyone. (5)

A further measure of validity is that, prior to the readings, these mediums know nothing about their clients except their first names. They have no prior knowledge of their situation, the reason for their visit, or whom they hope to contact. Yet, numerous details are provided that are impossible to know unless the information comes from those who have graduated from the earth plane.

Van Praagh relates the case of a woman named Marilyn who consulted him for a reading. During the session, he correctly relayed (6):

♦ the name Roger, her husband, who was always fussing with his reddish blond hair

- the cockpit of a plane with smoke and fire: Roger died in a plane crash a year before

- a happy anniversary wish from Roger: their anniversary was the week before

- a little boy named Tommy: her son who died in the crash with Roger

- Tommy's request to take down the *Star Wars* poster that hangs above his bed: he said he doesn't need it anymore

- Tommy mentioning the name Bobby, her other son, and saying he's not mad at Bobby for taking his red shirt out of his second drawer: Bobby was wearing that shirt today

- Roger providing the name of his buddy in the air force, where he was stationed, and his duties while in the service.

This level of information is not due to reading body language, fishing for general hits, or talking quickly. Even if these mediums knew who their clients were beforehand—which they didn't in controlled studies—they still could not conceivably learn so many personal details about thousands of different clients. Afterwards, Marilyn was convinced that Roger and Tommy were alive, well, and together in another realm. Her life was changed and she felt that she could live again.

At times, seemingly trivial details are very convincing to the client. Rosemary Altea told of one woman who hoped to get in touch with her husband. Altea described quickly making psychic contact with the man:

> I was amazed at what I saw. "I'm here," I heard him calling, and looked to the direction of his voice. Then I began to laugh. My poor client, obviously nervous and a little emotional at the prospect of hearing from her husband, must have wondered what was going on. I quickly explained, hoping that she would understand. "I have a gentleman here," I said, "but he is carrying two live geese, one under each arm, and he tells me that he couldn't possibly have come without them."

> My client burst into tears. "Thank God," she said. "I'm so pleased they are all safe." She told me afterward that the geese had been their beloved family pets. "Like children to us," she said. "My husband would often carry them around with him, one under each arm." (7)

John Edward relates the following story as told by Sue Farrell, whose twenty-two year-old daughter Tracy was killed in an auto accident. Tracy used to coach cheerleading and had been very close with one of her students. This girl heard a beeper going off at her home but there were no other pagers in the house except one that she hadn't used for several years. She figured the battery was dead but found it in the bottom of a drawer:

> She presses the button and sees a whole series of numbers. First was 07734, which she immediately recognized as the thing the kids do, where if you punch those numbers in and turn it upside down it spells HELLO. After that it said 112667. She knew it wasn't a phone number. So she's looking at this beeper, which hasn't beeped in two years, and she had been thinking a lot about Tracy, and about how unfair it was that she was killed. She knew Tracy's birthday was in November. She decides to look over at her dresser, where she's got the Mass card from Tracy's funeral stuck in the mirror. It gives her birth date. November 26, 1967; 11-26-67, the number on the beeper.

> So it says, 'hello' and Tracy's birthday. She freaked. She didn't know what to do. She calls me up and says, "Please sit down." She can barely get the words out. She comes over with the beeper and the numbers are still there. And the battery was dead but this message was there. (8)

The term 'channeler' is generally used to describe a spiritually sensitive person who receives information from advanced disembodied spirits. These sometimes exist as a collective group of soul energies, for example, the nonphysical intelligence known as Abraham that is channeled by Esther Hicks.

One advanced teaching soul, Emmanuel, is channeled by Pat Rodegast, author of *Emmanuel's Book*. The authenticity of this source is endorsed by revered spiritual teacher Ram Dass who has worked with them extensively. Emmanuel says: "This earth plane is neither the beginning nor the end of your existence. It is simply a step, a schoolroom. My friends, let me impress upon you how solidly you are planted in eternity, how brilliantly you can shine in your own physical world, how possible it all is, how beautifully the Plan is designed. In God's Plan no soul is alone. No soul is ever lost."

Further, Emmanuel teaches, "Death is like taking off a tight shoe. Even when you are dead, you are still alive. You do not cease to exist at death. That is only an illusion. . . Life and death should not be considered as opposites. It is closer to the truth to speak of dying as an entrance rather than an exit. . . It is absolutely safe." (9)

Some sensitives, for example, former White House and foreign correspondent Ruth Montgomery, contact spirit world through automatic writing. In *A World Beyond*, she reports these words by Arthur Ford from the other side: "Each person is a continuing entity through all eternity. No beginning and no ending. . . There has never been a time when we were not, and we always will be, even though in constantly changing forms and stages, for we are as much god as God is a part of us." (10)

A Legal Investigation of Paranormal Evidence

As mentioned earlier, in his book *Life After Death*, attorney Sidney Freeman presents much afterlife evidence including many cases about paranormal experiences of distinguished persons. I am grateful to Mr. Freeman and his publisher, *Kroshka Books*, for their generous copyright permission and refer the reader to Freeman's book for a full review of his collected evidence.

For example, Nandor Fodor's *Encyclopedia of Psychical Science* states that President Abraham Lincoln attended Spiritualist meetings and it was reported in the newspaper. As Freeman summarizes, "When confronted with the article—to confirm or deny it—the President replied: 'The only falsehood in the statement is that the half of it has not been told. The article does not begin to tell the wonderful things I have witnessed.' Through a medium, he received a powerful message to issue the Emancipation Proclamation. In the same session, while the medium, Nettie Colburn, was playing the piano for the president, it was amazingly lifted four inches off the floor. A colonel, a judge and two soldiers could not pull the piano down. Some mysterious force was holding it up." (11)

Regarding more recent events, Freeman tells of repeated spirit sightings after an Eastern airlines crash in 1972 and states, "Among the dead were the pilot, Bob Loft, and the Second Officer, Don Repo. On subsequent Eastern flights, the spirits of Bob Loft and Don Repo made themselves *seen* on many occasions. They were seen by stewardesses, flight captains, Second Officers, flight engineers and an Eastern Vice-President, *none of whom were clairvoyants*. After a thorough investigation, John G. Fuller furnished the details in his book, also made into a film, *The Ghost of Flight 401.*"

Freeman continues, "Fuller recited many amazing incidents which occurred on other Eastern planes after the crash. Among them were:

> A stewardess took a head count and found she was one over. She discovered it was an Eastern captain. She told him he was not on her list.

> The captain stared straight ahead and said nothing. She called the flight supervisor. He got nowhere. Then she called the captain of the flight from his cockpit. Half a dozen passengers watched the curious goings-on.

> The flight Captain bent over to talk to the silent officer. He froze: 'My God, it's Bob Loft.'

> In front of all the on-lookers, the real-life figure of Bob Loft simply disappeared." (12)

One approach to substantiating contact by spirits involves electronic recording of their voices. As Freeman describes it, "The most successful results were obtained with Dr. Konstantin Raudive, a Latvian psychologist. In the presence of guests, Dr. Raudive would record questions he asked aloud. After the questions, he paused and waited to hear answers. No answers were heard—either by him or the guests. But, miraculously, when the tapes were played back, answers were recorded on the tapes. Answers from whom? From his deceased relatives and friends. To avoid any charge of trickery, fresh, sealed, blank tapes were used and inserted by many different observers. A total of 60,000 such voices were recorded during the period of experimentations. The publisher, Taplinger Publishing Company of New York City, verified the facts by many different scientists before releasing Raudives' book for publication. It is entitled *Breakthrough, An Amazing Experiment in Electronic Communication With the Dead.*"

A high Catholic church official, Rev. Dr. Charles Pfleger, investigated these tapes and stated, "For some years now, we have been able to read reports in parapsychological literature about information received through mediums, indicating that the inhabitants of the 'beyond' are working on ways and means to contact humanity on earth. This idea is so alien to generally accepted views, that the mention of such an absurdity raises only a pitying smile; but anybody taking the trouble to study Dr. Raudive's experiments will cease to mock.'" (13)

A number of clairvoyants have been authenticated by scientists. America's most famous medium, Margery Crandon, was investigated by a panel of five experts assembled by the *Scientific American* magazine. Four of them summarized their findings as follows: "Some of the investigators have watched her at between twenty and twenty-five sittings without discovering any explanation inconsistent with her claims of psychic powers. . ." The fifth, magician Harry Houdini, had a long and intense history of medium bashing. He interfered with the display of spirit abilities, a fact attested to by his handyman Jim Collins after Houdini's death. Read Freeman's book for a full discussion about Houdini and *his* afterdeath communications. (14)

Several major churches have recognized the credibility of spirit communication and survival of death. In the early twentieth century, the Catholic church under the papacy of Pope Pius X, advised caution in uncharted waters but, as Freeman states, ". . . nevertheless admitted the validity of psychic phenomena and of external intelligences, based upon the reports of some eminent scientists."

Further, says Freeman: "An investigation of spiritualistic beliefs was undertaken by the church of England in 1938. . . The important majority report reads in part: 'Certain outstanding experiences of individuals, including certain experiences with mediums, make a strong *prima facie* case for survival and for the possibility of spirit communication, while philosophical, ethical and religious considerations may be held to weigh heavily on the same side. . . We think that it is probable that the hypothesis that they proceed in some cases from discarnate spirits is the true one. . . there is no reason why we should not accept gladly the assurance that we are still in closest contact with those who have been dear to us in this life, who are going forward, as we seek to do ourselves, in the understanding and fulfillment of the purpose of God.'" (15)

Ghost Sightings

The phenomenon of *ghost sightings* is another type of paranormal evidence that consciousness survives physical death. Just one authentic ghost sighting indicates the existence of nonphysical dimensions. In the video documentary, *Sightings: The Ghost Report*, paranormal researcher Tony Cornell of Cambridge University states, "There's a lot of fraud in this, a lot of imagination, a lot of wishful thinking but when you strip that all out, there's about 20% hard core stuff that's exceedingly difficult to explain." (16)

Simply put, ghosts are souls who are "stuck", for a variety of possible reasons, between the earth and spirit world. Our prayers and firm reminders that their bodies are dead and it's time for them to enter the Light can help them move on. "Helen" from Germany shared the following fascinating story about such a spirit:

For 3 months after my son-in-law passed over there was an eerie sense of cold about the house. I heard heavy footsteps outside my bedroom window and encountered many sleepless nights due to being poked and pulled at. I knew deep inside who it could be but chose to ignore it and pray that tonight would be the night that I would get some rest. This was not to be and finally I had enough. I looked at his photo with tears streaming down my face and said to him, "Okay, baby, I know there's something wrong and I will find someone who can help so that you can be at peace".

As soon as I said that, the room felt suddenly warmer and brighter and a peace came over me that I can't really explain. He had passed over so quickly and tragically that he had unresolved issues and hadn't accepted his physical death. He only wanted somebody to help him and if I wasn't so keen on denying his presence, I could've helped him sooner. I found a medium to help send him into the Light. Those incidents never occurred again.

In the *Sightings* documentary, Kerry Gaynor, a paranormal investigator from UCLA, points out that seeing ghosts is not culturally dependent; this phenomenon has been reported in all cultures since the beginning of time. He states, "How do you turn myth and legend into scientific facts? Research of photographic evidence has produced many hoaxes but a handful of pictures defy explanation. Startling images, spectral apparitions—are these people from the past trying to make contact with the present?"

For example, a 1965 NBC news broadcast reported on "The Stately Ghosts of England" in which professional photographers set up infrared movie cameras in a castle with a history of ghost sightings. Captured on film was a shaft of light clearly emerging from one door, traveling down a short hallway, and entering another door. As one researcher stated, "All the lighting conditions were controlled, windows were blacked out, there was no possibility of moonlight or car headlights coming through. When we saw the stuff later, there was a shaft of light which to me is completely unexplainable." Thirty-five years later, this paranormal phenomenon is still unexplained.

My sister has experienced ghostly interactions several times. While staying at a bed and breakfast in Colorado Springs, a "ghost lady" wouldn't let her sleep and tugged at the blankets until Nancy told her to go away. The ghost was a woman figure with long hair in a long robe and no real details to her face. She wasn't scary, just there, floating—not walking. The next morning, Nancy crossed through a cold spot on the stairway but no one else felt it. The owners verified that the place was indeed haunted and were not surprised at all by her reports. They had felt the cold spot on several occasions and said it moved depending on where 'the ghost lady' was.

States Gaynor, "To ignore it (claims of ghost sightings) is to retreat into ignorance. To pursue it is to pursue one of the most baffling enigmatic mysteries that we have ever confronted about the nature of our being and, in so doing, I think we have an opportunity to take a quantum leap in our understanding of ourselves, indeed, in our understanding of reality itself."

He led a team of twenty researchers at a house where malevolent spirit activity was reported. The woman who lived there could see this capricious ghost. Whenever she said, 'There it is!' photographers took pictures but these always came out bleached completely white. After the woman verified that the ghost had left the area, control pictures were taken with the same film and equipment. These showed completely normal views of the woman and her house.

At one point, Gaynor and his researchers felt very cold air followed by a stench so severe that several people vomited. A series of photos showed arcs of light that were in empty space. That is, although the light appeared to cross corners of the room, the light was not bent and thus couldn't have been from an earthly light source. These photos were featured in *Popular Photography*, the only alleged ghost pictures ever presented in that magazine. Later, a ball of light traveled among the researchers who ducked and yelled, 'Oh my God!' When the woman challenged the ghost to reveal its true appearance, an arm, shoulder, neck and bald head appeared that all present reported seeing. (17)

Just recently, an AP story described ghostly events at Hampton Court Palace outside London. Closed circuit surveillance cameras caught an unexplained specter after investigating a fire door that had been repeatedly found open. The pictures clearly showed a full sized robed figure with an unnaturally white face opening the door. A palace spokesperson said staff members were baffled and didn't know who or what it was. Ghosts associated with Henry VIII's third wife Jane Seymour and others have been reported there over the centuries.

Conclusions and Action Steps

Mediums, channelers, and ghosts—oh my! Paranormal information is admittedly a controversial topic, but there is much evidence that at least some mediums can actually communicate with souls from spirit side. Belief in mediumistic abilities doesn't have to detract from ones religious faith. In fact, it only corroborates what great spiritual masters have taught over the millennia. Paranormal is better understood as *normal* expanded to its fullest possibilities. An open-minded examination of this evidence stirs up a lot of questions and provides many wise answers.

The sensibility of paranormal phenomena was beautifully described by Therese A. Rando, clinical psychologist and author of *Grieving: How To Go On Living When Someone You Love Dies*. She writes, "Studies find that over half of all bereaved people report some paranormal experience. If it happens to so many, it cannot be considered abnormal. That surprisingly high percentage is cited in several surveys on the subject, and is even greater among widows and widowers. . . . the fact that so many bereaved report that they see, hear, or in some manner sense the presence of their departed loved ones suggests it is an important component of our experiences here with our loved ones in the hereafter." (18)

Suggested action steps include:

∞ Read further from among the books cited

∞ Ask others if they have experienced any paranormal events

∞ If interested, consider a visit to a reputable medium or psychic

∞ Discuss these topics with others in discussion groups

Benefit ∞ 5

More peace and acceptance about life's inevitable changes such as aging, children growing up, bodily degeneration, and so on

Change is the one thing we can always count on in life. Having a strong foundation of spiritual faith and knowledge helps us skate through challenges that inevitably surface. Well established roots help us bend, not break, when winds of change become fierce.

Yesterday, one of my neighbor's trees blew over. His huge pine tree was in a low area that collected water. As such, it didn't have to put down deep roots. When strong winds came along, it fell over.

Have you ever felt like you've fallen over? How long did it take you to get back up? Did you learn lessons that you wouldn't have otherwise?

Going through the years brings a predictable set of changes: outward physical changes, children growing up, a certain amount of bodily degeneration, and other minor transitions.

I'm not talking about major suffering like death, divorce, relationship breakups, financial loss, serious illness and others here. We've already discussed those.

Coping with even the relatively minor changes that accompany life is not easy. Last year, our younger daughter went away to college. My heart ached as I saw her empty room and didn't see her in front of the bathroom mirror for hours. For years, I had eagerly anticipated sleeping in instead of fixing her breakfast and helping her off to school, but now I missed it.

As my body begins its fifth decade, wrinkles, skin spots, white hairs and baldness have become all too familiar. These are minor things when we're primarily identified with our spiritual essence, but they're still tough to encounter. Recently while driving, I glanced in the rearview mirror and automatically thought, "That looks like my grandpa." Then I cringed when I realized it was me.

Parenthetically, the fact that most people feel young inside despite outward aging is, I believe, due to the fact that our real selves do not age. Our souls are spiritually immortal even though they are housed in a physically mortal package.

Changes that accompany aging cause us to look at life differently than when we were youthful. Once we've discovered our true roots—as magnificent and imperishable spiritual beings—we can better withstand the winds of life's challenges. The wise person prepares him or herself in advance and uses enlightenment to deal with changes.

We, as souls, came to this unique planet to build strong character. Handling the minor and especially the major changes here results in greater patience, love, wisdom and other priceless attributes. These qualities are well worth the price and bring us closer to God.

Most people have wondered why there's so much suffering and why God would allow even relatively minor adversity. Simply put, we cause much of our own suffering by inappropriate thoughts, words, and deeds toward ourselves and others. The rest is created by excessive attachment to the illusion of physicality, by forgetting that our real selves cannot be hurt and do not die. That's why we suffer while going through perfectly safe and natural life cycles such as aging and change.

The second part of the question—why God allows it—is easy: we have free will. We're not puppets on strings or automatons. If Creator set everything up perfectly, there would be no room for choice, experimentation, or exploration. We would essentially be robots since there would be no alternatives from which to choose.

Life is a lot like watching a series of plays or movies. You would get bored watching the same movie every day. In much the same way, we as souls spend eternity going through a series of plays that let us explore, learn, serve, and enjoy. When one episode is over, there are countless others to co-create and experience. Much collective evidence suggests that this analogy is much more apt than many people suspect.

Finally, life's challenges build spiritual muscles—much like weight-lifting. As I review my life, I clearly see that some of the most important lessons occurred after suffering took me out of my comfort zone. When life is easy, we don't have to stretch and search like we do when confronted with intense struggles. How much strength would I develop if I went to the gym and the other athletes said, "You take it easy today, Mark. Have a seat and we'll do the lifting." It's the same way in life.

Knowing this will hopefully help you enjoy the show, increase in godliness, and keep it all in perspective—no matter what minor or major transitions you may face.

Input From Religions And Spirituality

I remember going to Sunday school as a child and singing great hymns like "Jesus Loves Me" and "This Is My Father's World." Then we went upstairs for the church service and heard hideous scripture readings about a fearsome God and lakes of fire for the unbelieving and unrepentant. Even at that young age, I remember thinking, "Is this the same guy we were singing about downstairs?"

After studying various religious and spiritual sources for many years, I am personally comfortable with the saying 'Truth is one, paths are many'.

To differentiate between religious and spirituality input, the former refers to information from established groups with set doctrines that often date back many centuries or millennia. At its best, religion provides guidance, support, and loving service to many persons. At times, however, it impedes newer understandings, controls and restricts its members, and condemns those outside that religion.

Spirituality, on the other hand, is comprised of less concretized approaches to knowing and serving the Ultimate. Spiritual traditions are more open and dynamic in their interpretations and principles. This approach recognizes that all people receive Divine grace and celebrates—not criticizes—differences.

Religious and spiritual orientations are not mutually exclusive and can certainly be synthesized.

There are over 3000 different religions and denominations; they obviously can't all be the *only true way* to salvation. As such, in this section I will present a cross-section of various religious and spiritual viewpoints about afterlife and immortality of the soul. Each religion has more open or *esoteric*—as opposed to orthodox or exoteric—denominations that, in my opinion, offer wiser teachings. I will draw primarily from these esoteric views.

The Nature of God

The nature of God is discussed first since human beliefs about this phenomenon vary widely. Much collective evidence indicates that God is not a big bearded man sitting on a throne in the sky somewhere. Humanity's spiritual growth has suffered for too long by making God in our image instead of realizing we were made in God's image as beings of Spirit. In theology school, God was defined as the highest power of which we can conceive. The greatest image of God is that of love, peace, justice, energy, beauty, wisdom, power—the Life Force behind all creation.

Joseph Campbell, a brilliant scholar, author, and interpreter of sacred traditions, states: "The divine lives within you . . . the separateness that is apparent in the phenomenal world is secondary. Beyond, and behind, and within, and supporting that world is an unseen but experienced unity and identity in us all." (1)

The following description of God is the most pure and beautiful I have ever heard. In *Destiny of* Souls, Michael Newton, Ph.D., quotes a female client who was one of the most advanced souls he ever interviewed during a spiritual regression. She described Oneness, the Presence as: ". . . it is . . . massive, but soft . . . powerful . . . yet gentle. There is a breath . . . a whisper . . . of sound . . . so pure . . . the sound creates all . . . including light and energy . . . the sound holds this structure . . . and makes it move . . . shifting and undulating . . . creating everything. It is a reverberating bell . . . then a high-pitched pure humming . . . like an echo of . . . A mother . . . full of love . . . singing to her child." (2)

These descriptions of God are, needless to say, quite different from those that many of us were taught at an early age. Do the words 'wrathful, judging, and fearsome' sound familiar? Some denominations still teach about a God of unfathomable love and then, in the next instant, warn that this same God will send us to, or allow us to choose, a fiery hell for eternity. Can you say 'schizo-phrenia'?

Clark H. Pinnock, theology professor at McMaster Divinity College, states: "How can Christians possibly project a deity of such cruelty and vindictiveness" as to inflict ". . . everlasting torture upon his creatures, however sinful they may have been." A God who would do such a thing is ". . . more nearly like Satan than like God." (3) I agree.

We need to reconsider our notions about God, to refute half-truths and mistruths that we were taught in the guise of truth. Many people were brought up with the notion of a vengeful God who watches our every step, ready to smite us at the least transgression. These teachings were the result of archaic patriarchal and fear-based misunderstandings, numerous changes, and political expediencies.

Rediscovering the original import of sacred wisdom teachings conveys greatly different meanings. Aramaic translations help us rediscover more accurate spiritual understandings from that pivotal time and place that so greatly influenced Judaism, Islam and Christianity.

Regarding the primary Aramaic meanings of the word 'God,' Neil Douglas-Klotz, Ph.D., states: "The root words for God are 'Eloha' or 'Alaha' from the Hebrew 'Elohim.' All these words mean unity, sacred unity, or one Beingness. The Jewish or Aramaic notion of the Divine is not a being sitting somewhere, someplace as in a room above us but a unity of which we are a part, of which our being is a part. Both Jesus and the Hebrew prophets before him shared this bigger picture of the Divine. That's quite different from our Western conception. Our problem is that when this conception was squeezed through the Greek language and thinking into Western Christianity, only a very small part of this meaning was carried across the language bridge." (4)

If you were taught notions about the nature of God that seemed bizarre, realize that the offending information was likely incomplete or incorrect. Some people are atheists or agnostics because they understandably find the idea of no God an improvement over the strange images we have been led to believe are true about the Divine.

Other people are thrown off by denominations that claim their view is the only right one and all others are doomed to hell. At the "God at 2000 Conference," professor of religion and author Marcus Borg, Ph.D., said: "I find it literally incredible that the God of the whole universe has chosen to be known by one religious tradition." He said all great religions of the world, including Christianity, Judaism and Islam, suggest God is an encompassing Spirit that is part of everyday life. He described this not as pantheism but as "panentheism," which views God as not only transcendent and beyond human experience, but also immanent, or dwelling within all of us. (5)

Rev. Matthew Fox is a spiritual theologian, Episcopal priest, founder of Creation Spirituality, and author of over twenty books. He rejects 'theism', the concept that "God is way out there someplace, as far away as he can get" and—like Borg—embraces 'panentheism', that "God is life *per se* life, God is in the midst of everything that's bubbling, everything that's vital. And that is panentheism, to see God in all things." (6)

In *Wisdom of the Ages*, Wayne Dyer, Ed. D., states, "Imagine being fully aware that you carry God about with you. If God is everywhere, then there is no place that God is not. And this includes you. Once you connect to this understanding, you regain the power of your very source. Rather than seeing yourself as separate from the miraculous power of God, you claim your divinity and reclaim all the potency that God is. . . . you are a principal work, a fragment of God Himself." (7)

Joseph Campbell said that humanity's search for God is encumbered by conceiving the Absolute as a personality. One important mystic who broke past this orthodoxy was Meister Eckhart who stated, "The ultimate leave-taking is the leaving of god for God." Campbell comments, "As soon as you smash the local provincial god-form, God comes back. And that's what Nietzsche meant when he wrote that God is dead. Nietzsche was himself not an atheist in the crude sense; he was a man of enormous religious spirit and power. What he meant was that the God who's fixed and defined in terms appropriate for 2000 years ago is no longer so today. . . The divine lives within you. . . . And what is God? God is a personification of that world-creative energy and mystery which is beyond thinking and beyond naming." (8)

This theme of God within is echoed throughout the world's religions as discussed by Jeffrey Moses in *Great Principles Shared by All Religions* (9):

♦ Hinduism: "God bides hidden in the hearts of all."

♦ Shintoism: "Do not search in distant skies for God. In man's own heart is He found."

♦ Sikhism: "Why wilt thou go into the jungles? What do you hope to find there? Even as the scent dwells within the flower, so God within thine own heart ever abides. Seek Him with earnestness and find Him there."

♦ Christianity: "The kingdom of God cometh not with observation: neither shall they say, 'Lo, here! Or, lo there! For, behold, the kingdom of God is within you."

♦ Confucianism: "What the undeveloped man seeks is outside; what the advanced man seeks is within himself."

∞ ∞ ∞ ∞ ∞

The Nature of Humans

A more accurate comprehension of God's high nature naturally leads to a fuller realization of our own. As humans, we are lofty creations and are each imbued with a spark—and the potential for a flaming torch—of the Divine within. This truth is difficult for some to hear so I will quote a number of wise religious and spiritual teachers. The very first chapter of the Bible conveys scriptural proof of humanity's spiritual nature; Genesis 1: 27 states, "So God created man in his own image . . ."

Psalms 82:6 states, "I have said, ye are gods; and all of you are children of the most High." The apostle Paul, in I Corinthians 3:16 asked, "Know ye not that ye are a temple of God, and that the spirit of God dwelleth in you?" In Ephesians 4:6 he says, "One God and Father of all, who is above all, and through all, and in you all." I'm pretty sure St. Paul wasn't from the South, so emphasizing the word 'all' four times in one sentence makes it pretty clear: God resides within each one of us.

O. Lazarus, in *Liberal Judaism and Its Standpoint*, summarizes a Reform Jewish attitude toward death: "There is that within us which is immortal and it is not bounded by time and space. It is this, man's soul, as it is called, which continues, so we believe, to live after the death of the body. To it, death is but an incident of life." Kabbalistic or Mystical Judaism also believes in the immortality of the soul of all people.

In *Discover The Power Within You*, Unity minister Eric Butterworth says, "You can never be separated from God because you are an expression of God, the self-livingness of God." Speaking of God, Alfred Tennyson wrote: "Closer is He than breathing and nearer than hands and feet." Meher Baba said, "To attain union with God is so impossibly difficult because it is impossible to become what you already are!"

The Christian mystic St. John of the Cross wrote: "Oh, then, soul most beautiful among all the creatures, so anxious to know the dwelling place of your Beloved that you may go in quest of Him and be united with Him, now we are telling you that you yourself are his dwelling . . . his secret chamber and hiding place." (10)

Enlightened denominations from every religion teach our essential oneness with the Creator. In Sufism, it is said: "I looked into myself and saw that I am He." The Hindu *Upanishads* proclaim, "I am everywhere, shining forth from all beings." Christianity says, "The Father and I are One." Islam states, "All is Allah." 'Isness Is, God is One, I Am That I Am'—these are various ways of stating there is no separation or duality in life. As Joel Goldsmith wrote in *The Infinite Way*, "That which I am seeking, I am." Any other understanding is an *illusion* that limits our perceptions of whom and what humans really are.

In *To Know Your Self*, Sri Swami Satchidananda wrote, "Know that it's not the Self that needs Yoga. It's always tranquil. But the limited mind goes through these practices to expand and see the Self clearly. Then, when the Seer sees his Self and rests in his true nature, he sees the *real face* which is never disturbed. You are the image of God. You are the Infinite by yourself. . . Remember the goal: Aim at something great. All of you can be Buddhas, Christs, Mohammeds, great sages, and saints." (11)

In *Prayers of the Cosmos*, Douglas-Klotz relates varied Aramaic meanings of the first line of the Lord's Prayer, "Our Father which art in heaven, Hallowed be thy name." These include: "Radiant One: You shine within us, outside us—even darkness shines—when we remember. Focus your light within us—make it useful: as the rays of a beacon show the way. O Birther! Father-Mother of the Cosmos, you create all that moves in light." (12)

Many viewpoints agree that the Light of God exists within each one of us. In Matthew 5:13, Jesus, speaking to the multitudes at the Sermon on the Mount, said, "Ye are the light of the world." He encouraged them to let their lights shine to glorify God.

Finally, some comments on our essential soul natures from eminent theologian, philosopher, and psychologist William James who states: "Only when I become as nothing can God enter in and no difference between his life and mine remain outstanding. This overcoming of all the usual barriers between the individual and the Absolute is the great mystic achievement. In mystic states we both become one with the Absolute and we become aware of our oneness." (13)

A full apprehension of our essential natures makes obvious the realization that we are immortal beings of light. Having discussed the lofty nature of God and humans, let us now explore the concepts of heaven and hell.

Heaven and Hell: States of Being

Heaven has been depicted in various ways by different cultures and religions. These concepts range from literal, physical states of playing golden harps along golden streets to more symbolic representations of inner peace and connection with the One. In light of collective and contemporary findings, heaven does not appear to be only a future abode—with its own address and zip code—for a select few. The evidence overwhelmingly indicates that heaven is an open-ended possibility for all, now and forevermore.

In *Let There Be Light*, Aramaic scholar Rocco Errico, D.D., says that the ancients considered heaven, which also means sky, cosmos, and universe, to be the habitation of God. In addition, he states, "The term 'heaven' was also used metaphorically in the Bible to express the idea of peace, order and harmony. . . . Figuratively, 'heaven' also means a greater consciousness, i.e., one in which thoughts of lack and fear disappear. Thus one can readily see that the term 'heaven' also depicts a state of being and not just a specified location." (14)

In Matthew 3:2 and 4:17, Jesus said, "The kingdom of heaven is at hand." In Middle Eastern formulations, the term 'at hand' was commonly used to depict something very near or inside, for example, saying God is closer than your next breath or your own hand. In Luke 17:21, Jesus also said of heaven, "Nor will they say, 'Lo, here it is!' or 'There!' for behold, the kingdom of God is in the midst of you." When pressed for details, Jesus likened the kingdom to leaven or a mustard seed—both which have vast growth potential. None of these sound as if he were describing a place in the sky—someday—maybe.

For many of us, our perspectives about the afterlife came from orthodox religious teachings about heaven and hell. Taking scriptures literally can be problematic because of extensive alterations via interpretations, deletions, additions, and translations. Political and church power struggles entered into the equation as evidenced, for example, by councils that voted on whether to include certain books or topics in the Bible. As a result, irresolvable conflicts—such as an eternal place of torment—are taught that freethinkers cannot accept and even children can't fathom.

An elderly female caller shared this vignette during one of my radio shows. At age ten, she attended a very fundamentalist church with her family. Upon hearing about God's unfathomable love in one sentence and an eternal hell in the next, she was understandably confused and upset. After the service, when the pastor asked how she liked the sermon, she said, "I don't believe in the hell part, God wouldn't do that!" The minister retorted, "Well, young lady, if you don't believe that, maybe you shouldn't be in this church." Her parents took her by the hand and told him, "Maybe we shouldn't."

Over the years, many older people have shared with me that they never could believe in an eternal place of torture for anyone. Such a concept blasphemes a loving God and scares many people away from seriously considering afterlife and soul issues. These elders have learned to let go of past fears, trust their inner voices, and nurture personal relationships with God. Doing so frees one from fearful, archaic, and misinformed teachings. Then the potential for heaven on earth now and always becomes more apparent.

Joseph Campbell states, "At the end of the Thomas Gospel, the disciples ask, 'When will the kingdom come?' And Jesus answers, 'The kingdom will not come by expectation. The kingdom of the Father is spread over the earth and men do not see it.' In other words, bring it about in your hearts. And that is precisely the sense of Nirvanic realization. This is it. All you have to do is see it. And the function of meditation leading to that is to dissociate you from your commitment to this body, which is afraid to die, so that you realize the eternal dimension is right here, now, everywhere." (15)

A firsthand experience of heaven, then, can exist right now. Loving, serving, and enjoying one day at a time is a key. Releasing fear and realizing how loved and assisted we are throughout eternity is another. Taking quiet time to remember these truths and live accordingly keeps us in touch with the kingdom moment to moment.

Aramaic scholar Dr. Douglas-Klotz says that heaven is, "Not a place but a way Creation can operate; a modality, the vibrating Cosmos manifest in an individual or group, that is, it can be both a personal and collective experience." The Aramaic word *shmaya*, he says, best reflects the concept of "heaven when one recognizes the Oneness that is the universe."

He continues:

Heaven is not a place in the Aramaic/Jewish conception. Heaven is a way of looking at life. So when Jesus or any of the Jewish prophets used the word heaven, they were talking about a vibrational reality. We can read this that *Elohim*—the One/Many—created the universe in two modes: a vibrating, wavelike reality in which we are all connected (*shemayim*) and also an individual or particle reality in which we all have individual names, faces and purposes in life.

It is not as though heaven is somewhere else or a reward we get later but, rather, heaven and earth coexist side by side in this way of looking at life. The whole notion of heaven as a reward or something that is above us or some place we go after we die, would be entirely unknown to Jesus and his listeners. It is not Hebrew thinking and only arises in a later interpretation of European Christianity. (16)

The astute reader will notice similar descriptions of reality in this quote and those of quantum physics. That such diverse—in subject, culture, and time— schools of thought agree so thoroughly lends additional credibility that these models of reality are accurate.

When I asked him about the concepts that heaven and hell are levels of consciousness, degrees of closeness to or separation from God and knowledge of our real selves, Douglas-Klotz replied: "This is close to the original Aramaic. The Christian concept of hell is not found in the Hebrew or Aramaic language. The word usually translated from the Hebrew as hell—'sheol'—means a chaotic passageway through which the soul passes after the body goes back to its various elements. The notion of hell as some sort of eternal punishment would not have been known or even understood by Jesus and his listeners. It was not in their native language."

The term 'a chaotic passageway' reminds me of the tunnel described by NDErs after a suicide attempt. Are heaven and hell, then, at least in part, what we experience when we have our life reviews after death or during NDEs? To that question, Klotz answered: "It seems to me that they are, simply based on the language. The word for 'death' in Hebrew, 'mawet,' does not mean the end or the finish of something. It means a passageway into some other reality. This passageway involves, according to the Hebrew Scriptures, a period of confusion and a period of sorting out." (17)

Again, these similarities between meanings of an ancient language and validated NDE reports constitute additional confirmation of greater understandings.

Reports from NDEs, authentic mediums, past life and spiritual regression subjects, and enlightened religious teachings agree. Varied meanings of heaven and hell include:

♦ Our states of consciousness now, our level of realization that God is all

♦ How we feel given the degree to which our lives are in alignment with higher principles or miss the mark

♦ What we experience, for varying durations, when we die and review how we treated others and ourselves.

Much evidence rejects outright any notion of a fiery eternal hell or eternal separation from the Divine Presence *for anyone*.

Even rapists, molesters, murderers and those who commit suicide? Just a heartfelt common sense about a God of love reassures us that *all people* can eventually choose to join the Light. This includes even those who are so grievously imbalanced as to hurt or kill others or take their own lives. Christianity is the only world's religion that teaches an unending place of torment and that is limited to only some denominations.

The best rebuttal to the erroneous notion of eternal hell came during one of my radio interviews on a station in Louisiana. An elderly woman called and shared these wise, loving words: "I have six children and I love them all. I don't always approve of their actions, but no matter what they do, I will always love them. I think that's the way God is too." That started a heart-felt discussion of more accurate understandings of what hell may be.

Universal Salvation

Enlightened understandings about the high nature of God, humanity, and heaven naturally lead to recognition of universal salvation. This concept holds that all souls can eventually experience a heavenly afterlife and literally see the Light. There are no barriers, including time, to God's love for all people. Universal salvation is rejected by relatively few, but inordinately vocal and fear-based, denominations that preach an eternal hell for those who don't believe in their way.

Fortunately, all religions have enlightened denominations and individual churches that recognize the depth of God's love, understanding, and forgiveness. Eastern religions and Native spirituality traditions recognize the inherent oneness among all creation that renders any question of universal salvation nonsensical. They recognize the connectedness and sacredness of all life.

For example, Unitarian-Universalism has long led the way in recognizing universal salvation as well as advocating women's rights, enlightened mental health treatment, gay rights, and tolerance of other faiths. Early members included Henry David Thoreau, Clara Barton, Ralph Waldo Emerson, Emily Dickinson, Nathaniel Hawthorne, Walt Whitman, Dorthea Dix, Horace Greeley, Susan B. Anthony, and Thomas Jefferson.

In the 18th century, before the two groups merged, Thomas Starr King said, "The one (Universalists), think God is too good to damn them forever and the other (Unitarian) thinks they are too good to be damned forever."

Dr. Benjamin Rush, a Universalist member, physician, and signer of the Declaration of Independence, stated: "A belief in God's universal love to all His creatures. . . God will finally restore all of them who are miserable to happiness." This was a remarkable statement in an age when belief in eternal hellfire and damnation was widespread. The belief that the whole human race will be saved was condemned as heresy by church councils in 544 A.D. (18)

Sixth century A.D. was the Dark Ages. Might it be time to update our theologies, especially in light of contemporary evidence that supports more enlightened views?

Jack Miles, Ph.D., former Jesuit priest, and author of *God: A Biography*, states: "Much that the Bible says about Him is rarely preached from the pulpit because, examined too closely, it becomes a scandal." He cites examples of God destroying most humans in a flood as described in Genesis 8, a race He had created and described as 'very good' just a few pages earlier. Regarding the wisdom of literally interpreting the Bible, Miles comments, "Myth, legend, and history mix endlessly in the Bible, and Bible historians are endlessly sorting them out." (19)

The Bible supports universal salvation in a number of passages. In Luke 12:32, Jesus states, "Fear not, little flock; for it is your Father's good pleasure to give you the kingdom." In I Corinthians 15:22, the apostle Paul says, "For as in Adam all die, even so in Christ shall all be made alive." As my grandpa Marsh used to say about this passage and the word 'all': "That takes in just about everybody."

Consider the Biblical story of the shepherd who leaves ninety-nine sheep to find the one that was lost. In Matthew 18:11 and 14, Jesus said: "For the Son of man is come to save that which was lost... Even so it is not the will of your Father which is in heaven, that one of these little ones should perish." II Peter 3:9 clearly states: "The Lord . . . not willing that any should perish, but that all should come to repentance."

Other Biblical stories reflect how highly regarded humans are by the Infinite. When the prodigal son returned from the 'far country' of distance from godly ways, he was greeted with a feast and open arms. The same applies for everyone—and God's plan is not limited to a relatively few earth years. As described in Genesis 1:31, after creating man in his own image "God saw everything He had made, and behold, it was very good." As discussed, Hebrews 2:6-7 states, "What is man, that thou art mindful of him? . . . Thou madest him a little lower than the angels."

Some reject the concept of universal salvation because it doesn't seem fair; it doesn't appear to sufficiently punish wrongdoers. Actually, there is an exquisitely designed system of justice. We reap what we sow. Those concerned about the equitability of Creator's plan can rest assured that evil actions produce punishment—not by God but by ourselves. We create our own heavens or hells via the summation of our thoughts, words and deeds. Our life reviews and even our future lives can be heavenly or hellish depending on how we live now.

Universal salvation doesn't mean that spiritually ignorant and negative aspects of humans will survive over time. Evil and incongruous energies will pass away, but God knows the difference between the doer and the deed. Those lower, limited, sinful aspects fall away, burn up, wither, and cease to exist. The hottest fires burn off the dross and yield the strongest steel. Similarly, life's lessons will ultimately teach us to embrace what—in our heart of hearts— feels good or heavenly, and to release the bad or hellish.

So in that sense, yes, there are hell-fires but not as eternal abodes for our souls. This explains the various "fire and brimstone" analogies, the wheat and the tares' metaphors, and other scriptural parables. There is a burning away of lower consciousness. Our real selves mature over time to become more perfect souls, more pure reflections of the Creator. All souls—in due course—will freely choose to come Home and enjoy their rightful inheritances as children of God.

At some point in eternity, no matter how dark our station in life, we all will embrace our true natures and accept the gift of universal salvation. That possibility was there all the time, just waiting to be realized, claimed, and enjoyed.

Thanks to the vast cumulative contributions of religion/spirituality, science, and firsthand experiences, we can increasingly comprehend this good news. In the long run, we each will reflect our underlying essence and rejoin the Source. As Trappist monk Thomas Merton said, "We are living in a transparent world, and God shines through in every moment. . . everywhere, in everything. We cannot be without God. It's impossible. . . simply impossible."

Religious Views

With this foundation of higher understandings about God, human nature, heaven, and salvation, let us survey first religious, then spirituality input. Each religion has its own description of afterlife and criteria for attaining a desirable outcome. The *Bhagavad-Gita* scriptures, from the oldest surviving religion Hinduism, date to several thousand years B.C. and contain written and oral records about the reality of the spirit world. The *Bible* describes afterlife survival by Jesus and his visits to disciples on several occasions after the crucifixion.

Significant commonality exists among the various religions of the world. Each has nuggets of truth immersed within culturally laden prejudices, political influences, and human induced inaccuracies. Thus, the best understanding of ultimate truths, it seems to me, arises from sifting through great religions for common threads of wisdom.

In his book, *The Perennial Philosophy*, Aldous Huxley described common findings in different religions as summarized by Dr. Willis Harmon: "When the various religions of the world and of history are studied, it is found they each fall into two types. First, each religion has one or more *exoteric* or public forms. These are what we usually think of when the term religion is used. They are characterized by their rituals, the architecture of their halls of worship, their revealed literature, and so on. But besides this, each spiritual tradition tends to have an *esoteric* or secret version, known only to an inner circle, and usually involving some sort of meditative discipline. The range of exoteric religions is fantastically diverse. However, all of the esoteric traditions are essentially the same—or, more precisely, appear to be based in some form of potentially universal spiritual experience. This common core has sometimes been referred to as the 'perennial philosophy.'" [20]

Harmon considers this philosophy to be compatible with science and describes these esoteric similarities:

1. The world of matter and individual consciousness—the world of things and animals and people—is the manifestation of a divine ground within which all partial realities have their being.

2. Humans possess a double nature, a time bound ego and an eternal self. This eternal self is the spirit, the spark of divinity within the soul. It is possible for a human being to identify with the spirit—the divine ground—that is, to recognize ones own divine nature.

3. The life of a human being on earth has only one purpose—to identify with the eternal self and so to come to *unitive* knowledge of the divine ground.

Another way to appreciate the commonality among religions is to compare various scriptural passages on the same theme. *Jesus and Lao Tzu: The Parallel Sayings* edited by Martin Aronson and *Jesus and Buddha: The Parallel Sayings* edited by Marcus Borg, Ph.D., demonstrate the strong correlations among these great teachers.

Observe the common threads among the following religious quotes about immortality and our interconnectedness with God:

♦ Buddhism: "Knowing that this body is like froth, knowing that its nature is that of a mirage, the disciple passes untouched by death."

♦ Sikhism: "The Lord is in every heart, and within Him is my home."

♦ Christianity: "You are gods. Those are called gods to whom the word of God was delivered. . . No one who is alive and has faith shall ever die."

♦ Hinduism: "Deep within abides another life, not like the life of the senses, escaping sight, unchanging. This endures when all created things have passed away. . . The individual soul is nothing else in essence than universal soul."

♦ Judaism: "The Lord is my shepherd . . . Surely goodness and mercy shall follow me all the days of my life; and I shall dwell in the house of the Lord forever."

I'm comfortable focusing on the common ground among religions because it's a historical fact that numerous changes have altered original teachings. In Christianity, for example, original

Aramaic meanings were often drastically different from the versions that abound today.

Douglas-Klotz says the Aramaic language that Jesus spoke was richly expressive and contained layers of meanings. Middle Eastern and Hebraic tradition held that sacred teachings must be examined from three points of view: the intellectual or literal, the metaphorical, and the universal or mystical. The tragedy of Biblical translation is that expressions meant to resonate many levels of meaning were grossly restricted to literal interpretations. Greek translations from Aramaic are part of the problem since the languages varied greatly and Greek never became the language of the native people. Hebrew was primarily a temple language at that time.

He states, "All the major contemporary traditions of the Middle East—Jewish, Christian, and Islamic—stem from the same source, the same earth, and probably the same language. All originally called God either *El* or *Al*, which means 'That,' 'the One,' or 'that One which expresses itself uniquely through all things.' From this root arises the sacred names *Elat* (Old Canaanite), *Elohim* (Hebrew), *Allaha* (Aramaic), and *Allah* (Arabic). If this simple fact became better known, I believe there would be much more tolerance and understanding among those who consciously or unconsciously perpetuate prejudice between what are essentially brother-sister traditions." (21)

The Infinite does not just reveal itself to a few men who started religions millennia ago. Contemporary religious teachers—in fact, all spiritual seekers— can have Divine insights. As such, I learn from my own inner guidance, contemporary sources of wisdom, *and* time-tested religions. Consider the following quotes from wise modern-day religious teachers:

- ♦ "Just as a little bird cracks open the shell and flies out, we fly out of this shell, the shell of the body. We call that death, but strictly speaking, death is nothing but a change of form." - Swami Satchidananda

- ♦ "I am quite confident that the most important part of a human being is not his physical body but his nonphysical essence, which some people call soul and others, personality. . . The nonphysical part cannot die and cannot decay because it's not physical." - Rabbi Harold Kushner

♦ "The body is only a garment. How many times have you changed your clothing in this life, yet because of this you would not say that *you* have changed. Similarly, when you give up this bodily dress at death you do not change. You are just the same, an immortal soul, a child of God." - Paramahansa Yogananda

♦ "I believe there are two sides to the phenomenon known as death, this where we live, and the other side where we shall continue to live. Eternity does not start with death. We are in eternity now." - Rev. Dr. Norman Vincent Peale

Spirituality Views

Numerous spiritual teachers and philosophers from all cultures further support the existence of an afterlife and our eternal soul natures. *Native or indigenous* cultures had well developed and quite sensible cosmologies. Missionaries from orthodox religions considered them pagan savages and tried to convert them, frequently with disastrous results. Perhaps more people are ready to respect and understand sacred wisdom of other cultures.

Shamanism is an ancient aspect of indigenous tribal spirituality. Throughout history, shamans have existed on every continent. Anthropologist Michael Harner, Ph.D., in *The Way of the Shaman*, states, "Shamans—whom we in the 'civilized' world have called 'medicine men' and 'witch doctors'—are the keepers of a remarkable body of ancient techniques . . . A shaman is a man or woman who enters an altered state of consciousness—at will—to contact and utilize an ordinarily hidden reality in order to acquire knowledge, power, and to help other persons." (22)

Numerous validated shamanic events occur in the anthropological literature. Empirical cases that emphasize experience are also common.

"Don", a participant at one of my workshops, told me about his personal experience involving shamanic work:

My father died when I was 11 months old, so I never really knew him. I do have several of his possessions including a tennis racquet that he used. I used the racquet when I was young and recently was debating about where to store it. During that time, I began to think more and more about my father. A friend told me about a Catholic nun who is a psychotherapist and uses shamanic techniques. I scheduled a session with her and my wife observed the whole experience.

The nun asked me if a loved one had died who might assist her in spirit during the soul retrieval session. I gave her my dad's name. At the end of the session, she said that my father's spirit was present and that he had a gift for me. She described him holding out his hand with a tennis ball in it! It was an older version, not one you would find in a sporting goods store today. There was absolutely no way that the nun knew about the tennis racquet—none! I can only conclude that, somehow, my father's spirit was present and wanted to contact me with a sign that only my wife and I would understand.

Native American Indian shamans have contributed mightily to the collective spiritual wisdom. Some of their language is enjoying more common usage, for example, 'Great Spirit' and 'changing words', which I prefer over 'God' and 'dying'. Tribal elders can now share ancient wisdom with all people and provide another perspective that is beautifully aligned with the perennial philosophy. My friend Rainbow Eagle of the Okla-Choctaw tribe has learned from elders and shares their teachings in his classes and *A Walk in the Woods* and other books.

One example of the simple but profound spiritual wisdom is evident in the words of Black Elk, a shaman of the Oglala Sioux, who in his later years often crawled on all fours to play with toddlers. "We have much in common," he said. "They have just come from the Great Mysterious and I am about to return to it." Before Europeans influences, Native Americans had no word for the concept of fear. They completely trusted Spirit as they traveled through eternity and experienced life's changes.

Ancient philosophers contributed to spiritual wisdom traditions still available today. For example, Epictetus, the Greek Stoic philosopher, stated: "You have a distinct portion of the essence of God in yourself. Why, then, are you ignorant of your noble birth? Why do you not consider whence you came? Why do you not remember, when you are eating, who you are who eat and whom you feed: do you not know that it is the divine you feed; the divine you exercise? You carry a God about with you." (23)

More succinctly, the sixth century B.C. Greek philosopher and mathematician Pythagoras said, "Take courage; the human race is divine." "Know Thyself" is an ancient aphorism over the temple at Delphi in Greece. This admonition addressed the importance of realizing ones unending nature.

These themes are echoed in popular Higher Thought/Transcendental philosophies today. Such ideas are not kooky nor do they stem from the occult. A study of history and literature reveals there is nothing new or demonic about such ideas. Religious historian Karen Armstrong says that the philosophers Plato, Plotinus and Socrates also encouraged metaphysical studies without orthodox religious involvement for enlightenment.

The third century Roman philosopher Plotinus described the goal of our spiritual quest: "We here, for our part, must put aside all else and be set on this alone. . . to embrace God with all our being, that there may be no part of us that does not cling to God. There we may see God and our self as by law revealed: our self in splendor, filling with the light of Intellect, or rather, light itself, pure, buoyant, aerial, become—in truth, being—a god."

This vision of Plotinus has been echoed in faiths like the Quakers who teach that everyone has an "Inner Light" that, once discovered and nurtured, leads the way to salvation and peace on earth. One medieval denomination, the Brethren of the Free Spirit, was based on the philosophy of Plotinus and held: "God is all that is, god is in every stone and in each limb of the human body, every created thing is divine. The divine essence is my essence and my essence is the divine essence. Everything that existed yearned to return to its divine Source and would eventually be reabsorbed into God." (24)

Joseph Campbell says that certain themes, some of which are pre-Biblical, are present in widely different cultures that were separated by time and distance. Such motifs include saviors of virgin birth, catastrophic floods, saviors who taught morality and who carried and/or were killed on a cross, and saviors who reappeared after dying. Another recurrent topic is that believers tend to elevate their great leaders into deities. (25)

With this information, says Campbell, we can better understand the underlying spiritual themes of each person's great potential. Exposed are the limiting effects of past church-political restrictions such as the proclamation by Theodosius I in 4ᵗʰ century A.D. that Christianity be the only religion within the Roman Empire.

Huston Smith, Ph.D., discusses the concretization process in religious institutions that tends to freeze, dilute, or distort the truth: "Lincoln Steffens has a fable of a man who climbed to the top of a mountain and, standing on tiptoe, seized hold of the Truth. Satan, suspecting mischief from this upstart, had directed one of his underlings to tail him; but when the demon reported with alarm the man's success—that he had seized hold of the Truth—Satan was unperturbed. 'Don't worry,' he yawned. 'I'll tempt him to institutionalize it.'" (26)

Smith notes that religious institutions are the product of imperfect people and, as such, consist of vices as well as virtues. He recommends sifting religious institutions for their truths that reflect their value as the world's wisdom traditions.

I am not criticizing organized religions, but it's a historical fact that significant change and blending in them has occurred over time. As such, I encourage people to trust their inner voices and evaluate other sources of spiritual wisdom. We can then perhaps benefit even more from the strengths of established religions.

Conclusions and Action Steps

Enlightened religious denominations and spirituality sources lend additional support to the idea of our eternal spiritual natures. Perennial wisdom envisions a never-ending chance for all of creation to recognize and claim their inner divinity. Much religious and spirituality evidence points to the possibility of an eventual heavenly afterlife for all—no matter what their track record on earth. What other outcomes can there be when we really fathom the high nature of God, ourselves, and reality?

Action steps to consider for this category include:

∞ Visit different churches, synagogues, mosques, or temples to gain firsthand exposure to different religious teachings

∞ Read texts by teachers of diverse religions and spirituality traditions

∞ Talk about these topics with people who have similar and different viewpoints

∞ Pray and meditate regularly to gain more clarity about your personal beliefs

Benefit ∞ 6

Feeling closer to and gratitude for God and the Heavenly Host

My home is nestled among the trees on five acres with a pond and many critters. Bluebirds, flitting about with their bright colors, are one of my favorite and I have five boxes up to encourage their stay. Last spring, I noticed one building a nest in a box by the barn and kept an eye on it: first a little well-made nest, then two small eggs, and later, the mother sitting on the eggs. A couple weeks later, after a bad storm, I discovered the roof had blown off the box. My heart sank as I saw two lifeless baby birds in the nest.

At first, I was angry at myself for not devising a more secure lid. Then I felt momentary anger toward Creator—what kind of world is this where such precious little ones die before they get a chance to fly? Asleep at the wheel again, O' Omnipresent, Omnipotent, and Omniscient One?

And then I remembered.

I remembered the newer, more sensible images of the Divine that have emerged from the cumulative evidence. God is not a big man in the sky who controls all events: "I'll smite this one, save this one, a miracle her, a disappointment for him."

I recalled the wealth of reports that God is, rather, a life-force, a power, a supreme intelligence and energy that creates, sustains, and pervades all life. God is an unfathomable depth of love light, peace and joy. The Ground of All Being is all and is in all. That includes you and me and those baby birds.

Having remembered, I gently scooped their shriveled bodies out and recycled the physical vehicles that their life-energy had abandoned. I cleaned out the box to prepare it for the next family. I breathed deeply, recalling once again how exquisitely and perfectly designed this physical experience is for our spiritual growth, experience, and service to others. Although we are spiritually immortal, physical life here can be so fragile and fleeting.

This distinction is so very important. Some people understandably reject any notion of a Supreme Intelligence because of all the suffering they see about them. I remember counseling one man who said he used to attend church every week, taught Sunday School, prayed daily, studied the Bible, and had a great personal relationship with God.

Then his young son died. Years later, he was a bitter atheist and scoffed at any idea of God.

It's important to realize that God doesn't make anyone, especially children, die at a certain time. The evidence suggests that we live in a free will universe and each soul gets to choose its time of coming and going. This makes sense and answers the mournful question, "Why did God take my little baby?"

To this question, well-meaning ministers over the ages have variously answered: 'God works in mysterious ways.' Or, 'God wanted to be with the little one.' Or, my personal least favorite, 'The child was used by God to save lost souls."

Needless to say, none of these answers are very satisfying to those who think for themselves. In all of them, God becomes a puppeteer or a capricious dictator who mandates every detail of human existence despite the immense pain and suffering involved.

To be fair, these pastors did not have the wealth of evidence that is currently available. As such, they offered faith, which is important, but is vastly stronger when paired with knowledge and understanding.

We each create the quality of our own lives. It appears that we—as souls—choose major events in our lives. As such, it's rather silly to complain about anything. That would be like ordering a certain meal at a restaurant and then complaining about which foods were served.

By the way, this 'predesign' model does not imply determinism since we can change our minds, make mistakes, or veer from the blueprint. Ideally, we choose and live in alignment with Spirit, but we don't have to. We need only read the daily news to know that.

Expanding our concept of God is critical for understanding the recurring theme in the collective evidence that everyone is a 'saved' soul who inherits eternity. When we view God as a judgmental, wrathful fellow, we fall prey to archaic, erroneous, and fearful images of the Divine. With this model, an eternal hell is a possibility and we wonder whether we'll fritter or be annihilated after death.

A more comprehensive and contemporary understanding of the nature of the Divine makes such fears ludicrous. When we really grasp how loving, forgiving, and understanding Spirit is, any questions about salvation and eternal life seem silly. We each are part and parcel of the Source. How can we ever be apart from It?

Sai Baba, a contemporary avatar living in India, knows and practices being the divine spark of God. When a Western journalist asked him "Are you God?" he gently responded, "Yes I am, and so are you. The only difference between you and me is that I *know* it, and you don't."

Let me ask you a question: how hard would you struggle if someone held you under water and you were running out of air? When you desire to know God and your true soul nature that much, enlightenment is not far off. Spiritual realization is a process, but you can make quantum leaps in that direction in this lifetime. You can increasingly grow toward fuller and purer reflections of your inner divine potential.

If you don't yet have a meaningful relationship with the Infinite, take a moment to pray for that intimate reunion. Spend time in meditation, in nature, or any other timeless activity that quiets the mind. Seek and ye shall find. Ask and you'll be pleasantly surprised to find the Presence within and all around. That knowledge will help you absolutely know that you are an ageless spiritual being who is forever deeply nestled within the heart of God.

The gifts of this relationship are many. Most of all, we can feel a heartfelt desire—not fear or obligation—to walk with Spirit in thought, word, and deed.

May we always deeply remember and vibrantly live out our high soul natures. May we fully enjoy all the richness of life, knowing without a doubt that His eye is on the sparrow, the bluebird, and everyone of us.

Peri-natal Evidence

While getting a bath, a four year old child begins to talk to his mother: "I remember when I was in your tummy . . ." He tells her specific details about events that happened when she was pregnant with him. Later, he also correctly reports what happened just before and after his birth: which family members were there, medical instruments and tests, and even what people were wearing. The mother is incredulous; she is sure that no one has ever told him these details. How could he know what happened when he was in her womb and just a newborn?

The term 'peri-natal' refers to the time period just before, during, and after birth. Research on awareness during the peri-natal period suggests that a wise and objective consciousness resides within the newborn baby. The peri-natal experience, abbreviated as PNE, is particularly fascinating because it points to a *preexistence* of awareness, consciousness that predates birth. NDE research has strongly indicated a continuation of consciousness after death; PNE research addresses the other end of the spectrum, the time period *just before* and leading into this physical lifetime.

Parenthetically, peri-natal findings further highlight the importance of regularly quieting the mind to more fully comprehend the breadth and depth of reality. Frontal lobe brain function is limited at birth and often hampered near death. This relatively diminished mental activity appears to enhance perception of non-physical aspects of reality.

In *Mindsight*, Ring and Cooper review peri-natal research and note an emerging picture of a dual nature of human consciousness. First, there is a *brain-based consciousness* that develops as the fetus and baby grows. In addition, however, a great deal of empirical evidence points to a *transcendent source of consciousness* (TSC) that "predates physical life and survives bodily death." The TSC is most apparent during NDEs, mystical states of consciousness, and peri-natal experiences, but is usually overshadowed by the brain based consciousness so predominant in our hectic physical world. (1)

To date, PNE research primarily involves gathering information using hypnosis to aid memory recall from the peri-natal period. Interviewing children who *spontaneously* recall these events is another source of data. Please bear in mind that most scientific researchers in consciousness studies prefer the terms 'mind, awareness, or consciousness" rather than 'soul or spirit.'

Research Evidence and Cases

Research by Helen Wambach, Ph.D., provides fascinating clinical information about the timing of the soul's arrival in the developing fetus. Dr. Wambach hypnotically regressed over 750 people and had them describe their fetal life. The existence of two separate but simultaneous sources of awareness was reported by 89% of her subjects. They identified more with the transcendent source of consciousness than with that of the growing fetus. Her subjects described themselves as *disembodied minds* that hovered around the fetus and mother. This consciousness could come and go and had a telepathic knowledge of the mother's emotions. Nearly 80% of the subjects reported joining their preexisting consciousness with that of the fetus just before, during, or after birth. Only 11% reported doing so before six months fetal age. (2)

In her book *Soul Trek: Meeting Our Children on the Way to Birth*, Elisabeth Hallett discusses verifiable womb memories that suggest consciousness extends beyond the 'cradle-to-grave' time frame. For example, she cites cases of midwives who received accurate communications from babies in the womb. This information, such as warnings of increased maternal blood pressure or necessary changes in positioning for easier delivery, is often clinically useful. Some nurses have also reported telepathic correspondences during prenatal appointments from in utero babies. These communications reveal important, previously unknown details such as maternal domestic violence, high stress, or history of abuse. (3)

The most impressive PNEs are those in which children *spontaneously* and accurately recall near-birth events. These memories that occur without the assistance of hypnosis provide strong argument that consciousness predates the physical body.

One documented example of a peri-natal memory is reported in *Babies Remember Birth* by David Chamberlain, Ph.D., who states: "Jason, a three-and-a-half year-old boy, surprised his mother by saying that he remembered being born, that he had heard her crying and was doing everything he could to get out. It was 'tight', he felt 'wet', and felt something around his neck and throat. In addition something hurt his head and he remembered his face had been 'scratched up'. Jason's mother said she had 'never talked to him about the birth, *never*,' but the facts were correct. The umbilical cord was wrapped around his neck, he was monitored via an electrode on his scalp, and was pulled out by forceps."

Dr. Chamberlain hypnotically regressed ten mothers and their children who had not been told any details about their births. He concluded that their reports were remarkably consistent and "dovetailed at various points like one story told from two points of view." Validated details included instruments used, people present, time of day, and other specifics of the delivery. The timing of various events was also reported accurately during these independent interviews of mothers and children. Chamberlain said that, considering all the facts, "objectively gathered birth memories appear to be genuine recollections of experience." (4)

Rev. Jerry Bongard, author of *The Near Birth Experience: A Journey to the Center of Self*, is a Lutheran minister and counselor with more than 30 years experience. During his work hypnotizing clients, he has found that they easily recall *in-womb* and *pre-womb* recollections, that is, remembrances of bodiless states before joining the fetuses. Rev. Bongard believes that support for the concept of pre-existence is strengthened by the significant therapeutic benefits of pre-birth memories in difficult cases such as post traumatic stress syndrome in Viet Nam veterans. These *near birth experiences* allow clients to see themselves as spirit beings, thereby aiding the acceptance and healing of past emotional and physical wounds. (5)

Regarding peri-natal research, Stan Grof, M.D., author of *Beyond The Brain*, states, "I have been able to confirm the accuracy of many such reports . . . [Subjects] have been able to recognize specificities and anomalies of their fetal position, detailed mechanics of labor, the nature of obstetric interventions, and the particulars of postnatal care. The experience of a breech position, placenta previa, the umbilical cord twisted around the neck, castor oil applied during the birth process, the use of forceps, various manual maneuvers, different kinds of anesthesia, and specific resuscitation procedures are just a few examples of the phenomena observed." (6)

In *The Mind of Your Newborn Baby,* Chamberlain shares the case of a child, Deborah, who described in fascinating detail the events during and after her birth. She related memories *just after birth* with comments suggestive of a preexistent mind or spirit. Her strongest concept of herself was that of an intelligent mind that knew a lot. She couldn't understand why the birth attendants just focused on her physical needs and acted like that's all there was to her. Deborah felt frustrated that she couldn't communicate her feelings and that crying was the only sound she could make. (7)

Chamberlain comments, "The evidence supporting a physically transcendent form of consciousness. . . suggests that *a separate transcendent source of awareness coexists with the fetal consciousness . . .a* close examination of published regression transcripts reveals evidence of two intermittent streams of awareness, one assuming an *in utero* vantage point, the other one located outside the body of the baby. . . " For example, children in Chamberlain's research reported witnessing the newborn from two perspectives: as the child and as an observer outside the room. They expressed confusion about this dual awareness and wondered how they could be on both sides of the window. (8)

In the following journal article account from David B. Cheek, M.D., a young child under hypnosis described an attempted abortion that occurred when she was six months *fetal age.* The child had not been told about the attempt and verification was obtained from the mother after the session: "[Subject]: It's before I'm born. My father is shouting, "I'm going to kill you.' (A few seconds later, subject began screaming. She pulled her legs up to her chest as though trying to get away from something very frightening.). . . I saw that button hook coming up at me. I knew my mother was trying to get me out. [Therapist]: Then what happened? [Subject]: Nothing happened—only a little bleeding." (9)

Detailed visual descriptions that are later verified as accurate demonstrate an out-of-body vantage point similar to those reported during NDEs. These intra-uterine visual perceptions are all the more impressive when you realize that fetal eyes are closed within the womb. As such, PNEs with visual validation literally constitute a *double-blind* study!

Dr. Chamberlain described the case of Loretta who, as a third trimester fetus, sensed her mother and father on the deck of a sight-seeing boat. The mother felt seasick and tried to steady herself by holding onto a rail and looking at an island. The father was worried about her and wanted to know if she was alright. The parents never told Loretta about this event after she was born yet she accurately described many details of their outing. (10)

Another suggested resource on this topic is *Coming From the Light: Spiritual Accounts of Life Before Life* by Sarah Hinze. She presents over thirty fascinating personal stories from parents who describe connections with their children before conception and during pregnancy. Interestingly, such prenatal communications also occur among adoptive parents during the pre-adoption period. (11)

What are the conclusions thus far about peri-natal research? Dr. Wade states: "When regressed subjects are able to give accurate, detailed visual impressions of events that occurred while they were in utero—as independently validated by third parties—there can be little doubt that some extra-neurological, extra-sensory form of consciousness exists." (12)

After exploring all available research on verifiable aspects of consciousness around the time of birth, Dr. Wade makes some fascinating conclusions, especially for a research scientist. These summaries include:

♦ Our life essence or consciousness precedes this physical life and survives it after death

♦ The maturity of this highly insightful transcendent source of consciousness is not directly reflective of central nervous system functioning

♦ As brain activity increases, awareness of the transcendent source decreases, perhaps due to interference or masking by increased left hemisphere function

♦ A greater access to the transcendent source of consciousness (TSC) is enjoyed naturally by some and may be aided by advanced meditation, NDE or other encounters with the Light, lucid dreaming, and other disciplines

♦ Entraining or harmonizing of the TSC and brain based consciousness allows a greater and more peaceful experience of both physical and non-physical realities

♦ The TSC survives physical life, but excessive attachment to material existence and tensions between the two sources of consciousness may necessitate reincarnation

♦ From a level of Unity consciousness, the transcendent and brain-based streams of consciousness operate as one. An enlightened being recognizes that any indication of separation is illusory and that he or she is always firmly embedded in eternity

Conclusions and Action Steps

Peri-natal research provides more evidence that consciousness is primary, that we really are beings of spirit, life essence, awareness—whatever you want to call it. This body of proof further indicates that the mind is more than physical and persists over time and space.

Action steps to consider for this category include:

∞ Ask your parents if you or your siblings made any interesting comments that might have been reflective of peri-natal memories

∞ Ask little children if they remember anything before they were born and then listen

∞ Reflect upon the twin consciousness model discussed and how that might have created any confusion or insights for you thus far

∞ Encourage others to be sensitive and aware of the arriving soul's and developing baby's needs before, during, and after conception and birth

Benefit ∞ 7

Appreciation for and optimal care of your soul's bodily temple

A dear patient from Thailand and I were talking. Her command of the English language is limited and mine of her country of origin is nonexistent. I asked her how to say "hello" in English. She replied with a word that sounds phonetically like "sawatee." When she said it, she instinctively put her hands together and bowed slightly.

This reminded me of the word "Namaste" which is a traditional greeting in India that means 'I honor the light within you; I recognize that place within each of us where we are all one."

I asked her if "sawatee" meant anything else besides 'hello.' She paused for a moment, trying to find the right words and then said softly, "I see Buddha." I was deeply touched by the reverence inherent in her words and demeanor.

Her words also reminded me of St. Paul's statement in I Corinthians 3:16, "Know ye not that ye are the temple of God, and that the Spirit of God dwelleth in you?"

The Spirit of God dwells within you, me, and everyone else. We each are unique and important beings—like Buddha.

It's difficult to remember and demonstrate this lofty truth when we are ill, tired, or depressed. Caring for the temple of your soul is an integral part of self-actualization and enlightenment. We each live in a totally miraculous universe and possess a similarly miraculous body. After a near-death experience, people often experience a renewed appreciation for their amazing bodies. They increasingly commit to caring for the bodily temple and treating it like the priceless creation it is.

Deeply realizing your soul nature has the same effect. When you really know you are an eternal spiritual traveler, you can better appreciate your temporary housing. Cherish the vehicle that houses your soul and treat it with gratitude and respect. *At the same time,* remember the relative transience of physicality and don't become overly concerned with outward beauty, youthful appearance, and physical wholeness.

The term 'optimal wellness' recognizes that each person has a different level of health and fitness. You don't have to be an Olympic athlete to provide the best housing for your soul. Do the best you can given your situation. Keep yourself as youthful, energetic, and strong as possible but realize that aging, illness, or injury might change your circumstances. Christopher Reeve is a great example of someone who took the best possible care of himself throughout a wide range of physical conditions.

Seven keys to optimal health include:

1. **Sufficient rest**, sleep, relaxation, and leisure pursuits

2. **Proper exercise** including stretching, cardiovascular training and resistance training

3. **Eating healthfully** with natural whole foods, excellent supplements, and lots of pure water

4. **Body work** that tends to the skeleton, muscles and soft tissues, and more subtle energy balance. Approaches include specific chiropractic adjustments, cranial adjusting, massage therapy, acupuncture, yoga, polarity, reflexology, and others

5. **Risk reduction strategies** such as optimal waste removal/detoxing, minimal alcohol intake, avoiding drugs and smoking, and wearing seat belts

6. **Self-actualization strategies** such as fulfilling life work, happy relationships, and a positive attitude for a healthy mental and emotional life

7. **Spiritual awareness practices** to cultivate a greater knowledge of your immortal self

My book *Radiant Living* supplies much practical holistic health information and techniques for optimally transforming body, mind, and spirit.

Follow healthy principles most of the time, but also enjoy an occasional break from your routine. Live as if you'll celebrate your hundredth birthday and—at the same time—as if today is the last day of your life. Adopt an optimally healthy lifestyle that makes you feel vibrantly alive now and in the years to come. Living well—an art few have mastered—is part of caring for the soul's temple.

Multiple personal challenges during the past few years tested my body-mind reserves. I experienced severe sadness, pain, loneliness, and discouragement. I could have easily sunk into major depression and self-pity.

With gratitude, I found that my spiritual roots and my body-mind practices held strong through the tempest of those simultaneous trials. The question, "How would an enlightened being handle these difficulties?" periodically bubbled up through more hopeless thought patterns and reminded me to follow the light at the end of the tunnel.

Over time, I was able to turn those formidable struggles into an even deeper relationship with God, the heavenly host, and my soul. I grew in compassion and empathy for the many human beings whose suffering makes mine look paltry. My ability to feel, love, and care deeply was heightened as I transmuted my own pain and sadness into service to others.

The keys to thriving despite tough times are many. Here's a partial list of practices that helped me: prayer, meditation, yoga, exercise, extra rest, friends and family, optimal nutrition and supplementation, body/energy work (chiropractic adjustments, massage, reflexology, acupuncture), embracing the pain instead of avoiding it, crying, and taking one day at a time.

I'm back on top of the mountain, stronger and more dedicated than ever to help myself and many others know and live their high soul natures. Taking the best care of my body-mind made the journey to wholeness much quicker and easier.

Going through the valleys of earthly life can be difficult, no doubt about it. But we volunteered for these times; we each have what it takes to sail through life and enjoy the ride.

We each really are eternal, indestructible souls who are part and parcel of All That Is. Optimal wellness helps us remember the wisdom of words like 'namaste' and 'sawatee' that denote our magnificent potential and sanctity.

8

Reincarnation Evidence

Four prominent men believed in reincarnation. It just made sense, they said, and explained many mysteries of life. It seemed to be part of a universal plan that conserves energy and knowledge from one lifetime into another. They believed that a series of lifetimes allowed attainment of perfection, and found reincarnation to be a guiding light in their lifetimes. These men are highly respected in American history, but you may not have known about their spiritual beliefs. Who were they? Benjamin Franklin, Henry Ford, Thomas Edison, and General George Patton.

Reincarnation is the theory that we live not just one, but many lives. These different incarnations can be in *formed*—with some type of body—or *formless* states. Souls can experience life on planets like earth or on more ethereal realms. There is much evidence to support the veracity of this view.

Many of us were taught that our lives began with an earthly birth date and will end in death followed eventually by either eternal bliss or torment. This conventional model described God's plan of redemption as a very limited window of opportunity: one lifetime lasting a few minutes to many years and that's it until judgment day. Then the big cut: playing golden harps or burning in hell forever. That's a pretty bizarre plan for even a deranged human, let alone the most intelligent, just, and loving Power in the universe. This model is like a kindergarten level of understanding reality.

Reincarnation is a vastly improved model for understanding the open-ended possibilities inherent in eternity. It offers a more comprehensive and sensible explanation of reality, a more forgiving and inclusive life view. To extend our analogy, this model of cyclical lifetimes is like a high school level of understanding. Reincarnation, however, appears to be only *relatively true.*

The most absolutely true description of the nature of reality holds that all life exists throughout infinity without separation. It's a dance of energy, God manifesting and changing reflections of Itself throughout eternity. All is One, with unfolding *perpetual change* within the constancy of life. Time and space are only relatively, not absolutely, real and all life is interconnected. This is like a graduate school level of understanding.

The model of reincarnation—with sequential past lives as a separate entity—appears to be only relatively accurate. However, even with its implication of dualism with distinct times, places, and separate entities, reincarnation is still an improvement over conventional teachings. It helps us understand that our real selves are eternal, that our essence did not begin at birth, and does not end with death. It captures the ever-changing and expansive nature of life. This open-ended concept allows for the eventual evolution of all beings without limitations of time and space.

The evidence for reincarnation is vast and varied. Categories of proof include religious and spirituality input, philosophical arguments, and clinical evidence. The third category is further delineated into the subsections of: classic proofs, curative evidence, similarities between lives, past life regressions, past life memories, and Dr. Ian Stevenson's research.

Religious and Spirituality Input

Many religions, denominations, and spiritual traditions have a belief in reincarnation. This enduring belief surfaced independently across the world among billions of people in every continent on our planet. Reincarnation is a major tenant of Hinduism, Buddhism, and Sufism—a mystical branch of Islam. This belief is also part of several Jewish and Christian denominations. Native spirituality sources across the world recognize the cyclical, unending nature of life.

Rabbi Zalman Schacter-Shalomi says, "In mystical Judaism, we believe in reincarnation. It's call *gilgul.* We believe each time we incarnate, we move a step forward. Coming down one time prepares me for the task I have to do the next time. Whatever I conclude in this lifetime, if I come back again, I can take up from where I left off—not with the same memory, mind you, but with the same traces and vibrations and merit and clarity and God-connection that I had. Then I can go farther in the next incarnation to provide more input. If I learned a lot this time around, I get to teach the next time around! If I did wrong this time, I may get a chance to fix some of the wrong I did." (1)

Jewish historian Simcha Paull Raphael concurs: "Reincarnation is at the heart of esoteric Judaism, called the Kabbalah." *The Book of Splendor*, a book of mystical teachings, also called the *Zohar*, is the principal text of the Kabbalah. "*The Book of Splendor* traces the cycle of death and rebirth, called *gilgul*, which means both 'wheel' and 'transformation.' It teaches that each incarnation is a unique mission comprising lessons to be learned, commandments to be fulfilled, and deeds to be performed to balance wrongs committed in former lifetimes." (2)

The Hindu scripture *Svetasvatara Upanishad* states: "This vast universe is a wheel. Upon it are all creatures that are subject to death and rebirth. Round and round it turns, and it never stops. It is the Wheel of Brahman. As long as the individual self thinks it is separate from Brahman it revolves upon the wheel. But when through grace of Brahman it realizes its identity with him it revolves upon the wheel no longer. It achieves immortality." *The Tibetan Book of the Dead* says, "Thine own consciousness, shining, void and inseparable from the great body of radiance hath no birth, nor death, and is the immutable light—Buddha Amitabha." (3)

Christian theologian Dr. Leslie Weatherhead states, "Can Christians believe in reincarnation? I think they can. That is to say, I don't see anything in this theory which contradicts the Christian position. In our Lord's time, it was part of the accepted beliefs of everybody. Indeed, it was accepted by the Christian church until 553 A.D. when the Council of Constantinople rejected it by a very narrow majority. And after all, five hundred million Buddhists and Hindus accept the idea of reincarnation. To brush away an idea tenaciously held by such an enormous number of our fellows, including some very great saints and scholars, seems to me a thing one should hesitate to do." (4)

In *The Case for Reincarnation*, Unity School of Christianity minister James Dillet Freeman says reincarnation is one of the oldest and most universal ideas human beings have had. He has written and lectured extensively about reincarnation in the hope that others will find meaning in what often appears to be a meaningless world. Rev. Freeman looks at reincarnation as completely compatible with the important teachings of Christianity. (5)

As described in *Many Lives, Many Masters*, Brian Weiss, M.D., found from his comparative religion studies at Columbia University that, "There were indeed references to reincarnation in the Old and the New Testaments. In A.D. 325 the Roman emperor Constantine the Great, along with his mother, Helena, had deleted references to reincarnation contained in the New Testament. The Second Council of Constantinople, meeting in A.D. 553, confirmed this action and declared the concept of reincarnation a heresy. Apparently, they thought this concept would weaken the growing power of the Church by giving humans too much time to seek their salvation. Yet the original references had been there; the early Church fathers *had* accepted the concept of reincarnation. The early Gnostics—Clement of Alexandria, Origen, Saint Jerome, and many others—believed that they had lived before and would again." (6)

There are several passages in the Bible that suggest reincarnation was considered as at least a possibility. For example, in John 9:2, the disciples asked Jesus: "Rabbi, who sinned, this man or his parents, that he was born blind?" A person born blind to learn from past transgressions could only have sinned in a previous life. Why would the disciples have asked this question unless they were familiar with the possibility of previous lives? An understanding of reincarnation helps explain another otherwise abstruse passage in Rev. 3:12: "Him that overcometh will I make a pillar in the temple of my God, and he shall go no more out."

In Matthew 17:12-13, Jesus said "'Elijah has already come, and they did not know him, but did to him whatever they pleased. So also the son of man will suffer at their hands.' Then the disciples understood that he was speaking to them of John the Baptist." In Matthew 11:11-15, Jesus said, "Truly, I say to you, among those born of women there has risen no one greater than John the Baptist. . . and if you are willing to accept it, he is Elijah who is to come. He who has ears to hear, let him hear."

Philosophical Arguments

In Western cultures, powerful taboos still exist against topics like reincarnation. Social and religious half-truths and mistruths are powerfully reinforced onto children who trust that power structures teach unbiased truths. However well meaning parents, teachers, and clergy may be, much evidence suggests that they are wrong about this one.

Young people who resist cultural teachings are often judged, criticized, and ridiculed. As such, those who believe in reincarnation are bucking societal sanctions that have been especially intense since the inquisitions and crusades in Europe and the witch hunts in America. Despite this and the lack of education in the West about reincarnation, a substantial number of people believe in it. Roger Woolger, Ph.D., states, "A 1982 Gallup poll, for instance, revealed that nearly one American in four believed in reincarnation while in Britain polls by the conservative *Sunday Telegraph* showed that belief in reincarnation by the general public had risen from 18 to 28 percent in a ten-year period." (7)

Throughout history, great philosophers and thinkers—along with a majority of the world's populations—have believed in reincarnation. Famous persons who believed in reincarnation include: Plato, Socrates, Pythagoras, Plotinus, Origen, St. Augustine, Cicero, Marcus Aurelius, St. Francis of Assisi, Hume, Kant, Hegel, Schopenhauer, Nietzsche, William James, Henri Bergson, Goethe, Hugo, Sand, Blake, Wordsworth, Whitman, Shelley, Kipling, Voltaire, Tennyson, Browning, Alcott, Emerson, Thoreau, Poe, Whitman, Wagner, Leonardo da Vinci, Benjamin Franklin, Luther Burbank, Edison, Henry Ford, Edgar Cayce, and George Patton.

Consider these quotes about reincarnation:

♦ "I am certain that I have been here as I am now a thousand times before, and I hope to return a thousand times." – Goethe

♦ "There is no death, only a change of worlds." – Dwamish tribe Chief Seattle

♦ "As far back as I can remember I have unconsciously referred to the experiences of a previous state of existence." – Thoreau

♦ "Believing as I do in the theory of rebirth, I live in the hope that if not in this birth, in some other birth I shall be able to hug all humanity in friendly embrace." – Mohandas D. Gandhi

- ♦ "I know I am deathless. No doubt I have died myself ten thousand times before. I laugh at what you call dissolution, and I know the amplitude of time." – Walt Whitman

- ♦ "My doctrine is: Live so that thou mayest desire to live again – that is thy duty – for in any case thou wilt again!" – Nietzsche

- ♦ "It is not more surprising to be born twice than once; everything in nature is resurrection." – Voltaire

- ♦ "Forget not that I shall come back to you . . . A little while, a moment of rest upon the wind, and another woman shall bear me." - Kahlil Gibran

- ♦ "It is the secret of the world that all things subsist and do not die, but only retire a little from sight and afterwards return again." - Ralph Waldo Emerson

Binder and Hogshire state that Henry Ford believed in reincarnation: "It was, he said, the inescapable conclusion he had reached after giving it the same kind of hard analysis he gave to automobile manufacturing. For him, it helped make sense of mankind's recurring question: Why are we here? Ford said, 'Religion offered nothing to the point for me. When I discovered reincarnation, it was as if I had found a universal plan. . . . Genius is experience. Some seem to think that it is a gift or a talent, but it is the fruit of long experience in many lives. Some are older souls than others, and so they know more.'"

Benjamin Franklin also concluded that reincarnation offered the only rational explanation for life on earth: "When I see nothing annihilated and not a drop of water wasted, I cannot suspect the annihilation of souls, or believe that God will suffer the daily waste of millions of minds ready made that now exist, and put Himself to the continual trouble of making new ones. Thus, finding myself to exist in the world, I believe I shall, in some shape or other, always exist; and, with all the inconveniences human life is liable to, I shall not object to a new edition of mine, hoping, however, that the mistakes of the last may be corrected." (8)

World War II hero General George Patton, as hardheaded and down to earth as they come, also came to believe that we live over and over again. For him, the idea of multiple lifetimes served as his guiding light in his brilliant military career. He also offered stunning proof that his claims were true. In North Africa for the first time, Patton led others to little-known Roman ruins, the site of an ancient battlefield and said that he had been there before with the Roman Army.

Edgar Cayce was an orthodox Christian Sunday school teacher when he began giving psychic readings while in a sleeping trance. From this deep state, Cayce accessed other sources of wisdom and shared teachings from his soul's accumulated lessons over many lifetimes. These understandings included the concept of reincarnation as described in *Edgar Cayce On Reincarnation* by Noel Langley and other books.

Cycles in nature logically suggest a similar series of life stages for humans beyond death. Consider nature's seasons, ocean tides, sunrise and sunset, lunar stages and metamorphoses of moths and butterflies. Surely humans have as much a chance to return again, albeit in a different form. Look at the stages between physical birth and death: infancy, childhood, adolescence, adulthood, and the senior years. Why shouldn't this succession of stages continue after death?

Another philosophical argument for reincarnation is the vastness of the universe. Astronomers report hundreds of billions of stars in each galaxy and hundreds of billions of galaxies in this universe. Given the magnitude of creation, isn't it conceivable there are more options than just one earthly life, then heaven or hell for eternity? It's rather closed minded to rule out the possibility of other lives. As Eleanor Roosevelt pointed out, the idea of being born *again* doesn't seem any more fantastic than being born this time.

A cyclical system like reincarnation is the only way I can understand the paradox of an omniscient/omnipresent/omnipotent God *and* the multitude of sufferings on earth. Creator allows freedom of choice even when our choices result in suffering for self and others. But earthly sufferings that seem so great to us last only a blink of an eye when compared to eternity. Spiritual immortality allows us to learn even from suffering and death while eventually making better distinctions about right living.

The statement 'we all are created equal' is a cruel joke from a purely earthly perspective since a great and seemingly unjust array of inequities exists. From a *spiritual viewpoint*, however, each person *is* created equal. Much evidence suggests that we each are indestructible beings of energy, inseparable from and made in the image of the Creator. Only from this viewpoint can earthly events make sense.

For example, if this life is all there is, what about criminals and societal offenders who get off scot-free? What about those who don't seem to get a fair shake—children who die young, the retarded, addicts, and those who suffer greatly? If we have only this one chance, justice does not always prevail and many people have a valid grievance.

While we're examining apparent injustices, are we really to believe that our short lives on earth determine our fate forever? That those relatively few years—with all the confusion, temptation, fear, and ignorance on earth—determine whether we frolic in heaven or roast in hell for eternity? An all loving and wise Creator can surely do better than that. Reincarnation is the *great equalizer* that explains apparent human injustices and makes more sense of suffering.

Of life's apparent inequities, Rev. James D. Freeman says, "The only reasonable way I can explain this, unless I believe the whole thing has no meaning and is an accident, is to believe in reincarnation. . . because I believe in God and believe that He's love and intelligence, I also believe I'm growing to be the spiritual being He made me to be. I have lived before and I will live again. My life is what it is now because of what I was in former lives, and my future life will be what it will be because of what I am now. . . To me it's the only way you can make this life make sense." (9)

A cyclical series of lives also provides a variety of experiences. Imagine watching the same movie day after day for millennia; how boring and limiting would that be? I remember sitting in church at age ten and thinking that playing golden harps in heaven would get tedious after a while. Reincarnation provides various and unending opportunities for exploration, service, growth, and enjoyment.

An understanding of reincarnation helps explain other philosophical quandaries. For example, altruistic acts that endanger ones life have long puzzled social scientists. The instinct for survival is usually the strongest yet many persons have risked or lost their lives trying to save complete strangers. Perhaps in a moment of unselfish passion and recognition of human need, the higher self shines through and overcomes basic instincts. That is, unconscious memories of the soul's imperishability might overcome the rescuer's ego-based concern for self-preservation. Or perhaps the person in need wasn't a "complete stranger" but was connected through one or more past lives.

Consider the attraction between couples of widely varying age, appearance, or interests. Perhaps they unconsciously recognize a familiar soul in each other, thereby rendering physical criteria less important. Other couples who stay together despite marked unhappiness may need to heal quarrelsome patterns that have resurfaced over lifetimes.

Clinical Evidence

Classic Proofs

The phenomena of child prodigies, familiarity, and xenoglossy have long been identified across cultures and further suggest the existence of previous lifetimes.

Over time, a number of *child prodigies* have demonstrated amazing abilities in mathematics, music, and other fields. Some have displayed virtuoso musical abilities despite little or no practice at that instrument. Mozart, for example, composed a concerto at age four.

In *How To Know God*, Deepak Chopra, M.D., describes the most famous musical prodigy of the present generation, Russian pianist Evgeny Kissin. His mother vividly recalls that her one-year-old hummed Bach inventions in perfect pitch. "And as soon as Evgeny could toddle, he made his way to the family piano and began to pick out the same Bach exercises that he had heard his older sister practicing. These were just the first signs exhibited by a child prodigy who was composing music at six and performing both Chopin piano concertos in a single concert at age of thirteen—a prodigious feat even for an accomplished virtuoso."

Chopra continues, "People who spend time with geniuses and prodigies often find them unearthly, somehow preternatural, as if a very old soul has been confined to a new body and yet brings in experience far beyond what that body could have known. It is easy to credit that some kind of former life is casting its influence on the present. Speaking of his own experience, one musical prodigy stated, 'It is as if I am playing from outside my own consciousness. The music comes through me. I am the conduit, not the source." (10)

Familiarity is another occurrence that is puzzling unless a greater nonphysical awareness exists across time and space. Familiarity includes having detailed knowledge of a particular historical period, place or person one has never studied, visited or met. For example, some people, upon arriving at a country or city for the first time, intimately know directions and locations of landmarks. Even more common is the occurrence of meeting someone for the first time and having a strong sense of having known each other before. This may partially account for the instant fondness or dislike we feel toward new acquaintances. Familiarity is often exhibited during a past life regression or memories of past lives.

Xenoglossy is the phenomenon of being able to speak one or more languages fluently without any exposure to them in the present lifetime. In *Reincarnation: The Phoenix Fire Mystery*, Cranston and Head relate the story of Dr. Marshall McDuffie, a prominent New York physician, and his wife Wilhelmina whose ". . . twin baby boys were found to be conversing among themselves in some unknown vernacular. The children were eventually taken to the foreign language department of Columbia University, but none of the professors present could identify their speech. However, a professor of ancient languages happened to pass by and was amazed to discover that the babies were speaking Aramaic, a language current at the time of Christ." (11)

Dr. Frederick Lenz describes a mother's account of her daughter's nighttime xenoglossy. The parents were awakened by the sound of a strange voice coming from the bedroom of their six-year-old daughter. They found her talking in her sleep, speaking rapidly in French. The mother stated, "My daughter is six and has never been outside this country and has never been exposed to anyone who speaks French." When this happened several nights in a row, the parents taped the conversation and took it to a local French teacher. "She listened to it and told us that the little girl (our daughter) on the tape was looking for her mother, who she had been separated from when her village was attacked by the Germans. She said the little girl seemed to be lost and, judging from her tone of voice, was very distressed. It is my feeling that our daughter lived before in a village in France and probably died in one of the world wars." (12)

Curative Evidence

Healing of various emotional and physical disorders by past life regression or spontaneous recall contributes additional evidence for reincarnation. The existence of unexplainable phobias, for example, the irrational fear of guillotines, is an indication of negative tension carried over from past lives. Cures of these difficult disorders are especially impressive since they are often spontaneous and occur after numerous orthodox approaches have failed. These therapeutic recoveries are also often total and lasting.

Hans Holzer, Ph.D., describes Israeli bio-energetic healer Ze'ev Kolman's abilities to know and use past-life information. Says Holzer, "Increasing numbers of doctors take quite seriously symptoms caused by situations in previous lives that are unknown to the sufferer, because there are positive results to back them up. When the patient understands the origin of the affliction, it appears that the matter is solved. . ." (13)

Michael Newton, Ph.D., resisted requests for past life regressions until he worked with a man who suffered with severe pain: "This client complained of a lifetime of chronic pain on his right side. . . . I eventually uncovered his former life as a World War I soldier who was killed by a bayonet in France, and we were able to eliminate the pain altogether. . . . I came to appreciate just how therapeutically important the link is between the bodies and events of our former lives and who we are today." (14)

Carol Bowman, M.A., describes a curative case reported by Patricia Austrian who believes a potentially fatal tumor in her child Edward was cured when he remembered a past life. From the time he could first talk, little Edward would point to his throat and say, "My shot hurts, my shot hurts!" He had trouble swallowing and his parents thought he was comparing his throat pain to getting an injection. A specialist found a large cyst in his throat and scheduled a tonsillectomy first before removing the growth several weeks later. Just after the tonsillectomy, Edward said the "shot" was gone. His parents assumed he was delirious from the anesthetic.

Bowman writes, "Then his utterances became even stranger. He told them that *when he was big before,* he had been a soldier in France named Walter. . . a bullet hit him from behind and lodged in his throat. Four-year-old Edward then gave what was, his physician father attested later, a clinically accurate description of dying from a bullet wound in the throat—grisly details that very few adults, let alone a four-year-old, would know. He repeated his story, word for word, over the next few days." The parents were puzzled as to how their child would know such accurate details. Within three days, the growth had completely disappeared. The surgeon was amazed by his spontaneous remission and expected it to return but it hadn't ten years later. (15)

Similarities Between Lives

In his book, *Where Reincarnation and Biology Intersect*, Ian Stevenson, M.D., discusses the occurrence of similarities between lives. He shows pictures of people in present and purported past lives and notes the physical resemblances including past life injuries and present day birth marks or deformities. I'll discuss Stevenson's work more fully later in this chapter.

Walter Semkiw, M.D., has also researched this phenomenon extensively. He holds that, from lifetime to lifetime, people tend to exhibit similar physical characteristics and persistent personality traits. Many of the physical resemblances Semkiw shows are striking and eerily similar. Moreover, he has identified similar modes of expression, such as writing styles. Symbols and synchronistic events that reflect important features of a person's past lives, he claims, are often found in a person's current lifetime. Dr. Semkiw uses public records and historical archives to document these parallel features.

His book, *Return of the Revolutionaries*, shows numerous sets of pictures of people as they look now and as they did in alleged past lives. Some of them discovered their past-life connections by spontaneous memories, dreams, or input from mediums or psychics. Dr. Semkiw has investigated a number of these in depth and considers their cases to be authentic. The subject of one of his cases, Nobel Laureate Kary Mullis, Ph.D., has proposed testing of current and alleged past life tissue samples for DNA comparison. (16)

Past Life Regressions

In this subsection, I will discuss *hypnotically induced* past life regressions (PLRs) as opposed to spontaneous past life memories. PLRs are fragments of supposed past lives experienced while the subject is under hypnosis. The deeply relaxed hypnotic state facilitates a calm but clear state of mind that results in less mental chatter. Quieting the brain's frenetic analysis and worrying apparently allows awareness of other information not usually accessible in the waking state.

To skeptics who charge that PLR subjects are deliberately lying about their experiences, Edith Fiore, Ph.D., author of *You Have Been Here Before,* responds, "If so, most should be nominated for Academy awards. I have listened to and watched people in past-life regressions under hypnosis for thousands of hours. I am convinced there is no deliberate, nor conscious attempt to deceive. The tears, shaking, flinching, smiling, gasping for breath, groaning, sweating and other physical manifestations are all too real." (17)

Dr. Weiss says that he has received thousands of phone calls and letters from psychiatrists, psychologists, and other therapists who have done past life regressions for up to twenty years. He states, "The letters describe detailed accounts of past-life recall, of patients recalling names, dates, and details of lifetimes in other cities, countries, or continents. Some patients have found their 'old' names in the official records of places they have never even heard of, let alone visited, in this lifetime. Some have found their own tombstones." (18)

As described in *Reliving Past Lives,* Helen Wambach, Ph.D., evaluated over a thousand cases of detailed past lives and stated, "I reasoned that if past-life recall were fantasy, my subjects would include material in their regressions that I could prove could not have been true. They might have seen anachronisms of one kind or another—clothing and architecture that was completely wrong for the time period and place they had chosen—or a climate and landscape that would not match the map they flashed on. . . To my surprise, I found only eleven data sheets out of the 1,088 I had collected that showed clear evidence of discrepancies."

Dr. Wambach analyzed these accumulated past life recollections and compared them for historical accuracy in the areas of social class, race, gender, clothing, diet, population ratios, and causes of death in particular time periods. For example, she found that 49 percent of past lives were lived as women, while 51 percent were those of men—just about what one would expect in a random distribution, not a hoax. She concluded, "All the data described in this chapter tended to support the hypothesis that past-life recall accurately reflects the real past rather than that it represents common fantasies." (19)

She also found that the number of lives reported around 400 A.D. was half that reported around 1600 and that this number doubled once more around 1850—duplicating exactly the actual increase in the population of the world. It is difficult, if not impossible, to believe that a group of randomly selected participants in past-life regressions could have co-coordinated their efforts to pull off such a colossal hoax.

Joel Whitton, M.D., Ph.D., is a professor of psychiatry at the University of Toronto Medical School and co-author with Joe Fisher of *Life Between Life.* They relate Whitton's clinical work with a client named Harold who, when hypnotized, described a former life as a Viking raider named Thor. Although he had never studied a foreign language in his life, the man spoke comfortably and confidently in a strange tongue that experts identified as ancient Norse.

Working independently, linguists who spoke Icelandic and Norwegian identified and translated some of these words. Several other words seemed to have a Russian, Serbian, or Slavic derivation and these were also identified. One language expert stated, "It would be appropriate for a Viking to speak a language which contained words and phrases of other tongues in that period. I would say this could fit the language pattern of the roving Viking."

During another past life recollection, Harold wrote what looked like a bunch of scribbles to him and Dr. Whitton. The alphabet he used was identified by researchers as a long-extinct script used in Mesopotamia. That language bears no relation to modern Iranian and hasn't been spoken for more than 1300 years. Of Harold's past-life regression experiences, Dr. Whitton states, "To me, the case remains one of the most convincing arguments I've seen for evidence of reincarnation." (20)

One final example of a PLR with validation features was provided by Dr. Weiss. Diane, an R.N., was unmarried and had been looking without success for a soul mate relationship. During a past-life regression with Weiss, she recalled an earlier lifetime as a settler woman who hid with her baby from Indians. To keep the baby quiet, she covered his mouth with her hand. Her baby, who had a crescent shaped birthmark beneath his right shoulder, died as she accidentally asphyxiated him. Several months after this regression, she treated a man with asthma at her hospital job. She nearly fainted when, while listening to his lungs, she saw a crescent shaped birthmark below his right shoulder. Both experienced an instant familiarity and connection that led to dating and a happy marriage. (21)

Past Life Memories

Past life memories, which I abbreviate PLMs, are another category of evidence for reincarnation. These occur *spontaneously*, that is, without the aid of hypnosis, while the person is awake or dreaming. There are many validated PLM cases in the literature.

The following past life memory came during dreams and waking visions as described in the book *Across Time and Death* by Jenny Cockell. As a child, Jenny had vivid, recurrent dreams of dying from a fever and leaving behind eight young children. She awakened from these dreams sobbing and feeling terribly sad and guilty about leaving them. While very young, Jenny began drawing maps and scenes of a small Irish village and continued to do so over the years. As an adult, she traced her former identity to Mary Sutton who had indeed died from a fever and had eight children. She traveled to Ireland and had emotional reunions with Mary's now grown children who verified that Jenny knew details that only their mother could have known. After this contact with her children, Jenny no longer suffered from the recurrent dreams, guilt, and sadness. (22)

A psychology graduate student told Dr. Weiss about an evidential dream that occurred when the student's wife was four months pregnant and the gender of the baby wasn't yet known. In a vivid dream, his unborn daughter told him her name, immediate past life, life purposes, and why she chose to be born to them. He awakened and turned toward his wife who said that she, too, had just experienced an amazing dream. While comparing notes, they were astounded to find all the details were the same. That both parents simultaneously and identically had the same dream strengthens the indication that an actual spirit visit happened. To further validate the information, a beautiful daughter was born five months later. (23)

Many young children have spontaneously reported past life memories. Carol Bowman relates another PLM case from England as reported by Peter and Mary Harrison in *The Children That Time*

Forgot: "Desmond had been playing with his toy cars on the floor when he told his mother, without any prompting, 'You know, Mummy, I went to Aunty Ruth before I came to you, but I didn't stay there very long.' His mother was stunned to hear her three-and-a-half-year old say this. Her sister-in-law, Ruth, had given birth to a stillborn son ten years before. But the family had a pact to never speak of it because it had been so traumatic for her. Desmond could never have overheard anyone discuss it." Describing his time in Ruth's womb, Desmond said, "One time I went to sleep but when I woke up again I wasn't with Aunty Ruth any more."

A final case was reported by Hilda Swiger, a grandmother from Florida, whose son Richard was killed in a car accident at the age of twenty-eight. Hilda dreamed about Richard often until her other son's wife was pregnant. When her grandson Randy was born, she felt an immediate strong connection and hoped it was Richard's soul that had returned. When Randy was two and a half, he found a picture of an angel that Richard had painted. He became excited and ran to his father, saying "Lookie, Daddy, lookie. Me painted this. Me painted this a long time ago." At age 3, Randy said to Hilda, "I was in your belly before I went to my mommy. But then I died and went to heaven and I saw Grandpa John. But I knew you needed me, so I came down here in my mommy's belly so I could be with you." Now, Hilda says, the entire family believes that Richard has returned as Randy. (24)

Dr. Ian Stevenson's Research

The massive amount of objective research by Ian Stevenson, M.D., is the most impressive reincarnation evidence to date. Dr. Stevenson's books include *Children Who Remember Previous Lives, Cases of the Reincarnation Type, Twenty Cases Suggestive of Reincarnation, Where Reincarnation and Biology Intersect*, and *Reincarnation and Biology*. The world's leading authority on the subject, he is the author of more than a dozen scholarly books and 250 articles.

Dr. Stevenson, who headed the department of psychiatry at the University of Virginia, has spent most of his sixty-year career perfecting methods for verifying the past life memories of children. His work is not better known because he writes for other academicians, a fact to which anyone who has read his books can attest.

He and his staff have compiled over 3000 cases from Asia, Europe, Africa, and North America. Nearly 900 of these are stringently verified and 35% of these have birthmarks or birth defects that match injuries from previous lives. Eighteen of these cases involve two or more matching birthmarks. Stevenson calculated the chances that two matching sets of birthmarks would randomly occur to be 1 in 25,600. The odds against this happening by chance eighteen times are astronomical.

Dr. Stevenson's stringent standards of research rely heavily on private, repeated interviews over time. He wrote a clinical textbook for psychiatrists based on methods used by attorneys to reconstruct past events as accurately as possible. He and his team investigate the child who remembers a possible past life and their families, as well as the family and circumstances of the alleged past life. Given the exacting methods of these professional researchers, it is virtually impossible for anyone to conceal a hoax—especially third-world villagers.

Here are three summaries of Dr. Stevenson's cases:

♦ A 3 ½ year old boy from India, Parmod, remembered owning a soda and bakery store in another town. He led his family directly to the shop upon arriving in that town and knew how to repair a complex soda machine that had been intentionally disconnected to test his memory . . .

♦ Michael, a 3 year old from Texas, remembered exact details of a fatal auto accident in his previous life. His recollection—although no one in the family had ever told him—was that of his mother's high school boyfriend who had died just as Michael described.

♦ At just 1 ½ years of age, Sukla of India cradled a toy and said it was her daughter, Minu. During the next several years, she remembered more details of her past life and her family took her to that village. Sukla directed them to her former home and enjoyed a reunion with Minu, whose mother had died when she was a baby.

Jenny Wade, Ph.D., notes parallels between peri-natal memories and accounts by children about past lives. She views such events as supporting an argument for consciousness independent of a physical body. Wade states that Stevenson's research has withstood every serious challenge to date because of the impressive documentation and rigorous scientific methods used. Especially convincing, says Wade, is the high incidence of birthmarks and deformities in this life that correspond to injuries in a former life. (25)

Of these correlating birthmarks, author John Algeo comments, "For example, a child may remember having lived another life including enough details about it (names, places, events) to permit investigators to identify the earlier personality. That personality died from a gunshot wound, and medical or coroner's records establish the location of the entering and exiting wound marks made by the fatal bullet. The child who remembers the earlier life has birthmarks on places that correspond to the wounds of the prior personality. Moreover, the birthmark corresponding to the exit wound is larger than the birthmark corresponding to the entry wound, just as the wounds themselves were, that being the normal pattern for bullet wounds. That is one type of case out of many involving birthmarks and defects." (26)

In Stevenson's *Reincarnation and Biology*—an eight pound, two volume work with 2268 pages—photos show rare birth marks or defects that correlate with previous lives. One Burmese girl, born with her right leg missing just below the knee, remembered the life of a poor teenage girl who sold roses to passengers at the railroad station. A train ran over her and severed her right leg. The girl made detailed statements and recognitions that convinced the family she was the reincarnation of the teenager who was killed by the train. She also had a marked phobia of trains.

Other examples of correlating birthmarks offering physical evidence of links to past lives include an Indian boy who recalled being killed by a shotgun blast to his chest. On this little boy's chest was an array of birthmarks that matched the pattern and location of the fatal wounds as verified by the autopsy report. Another shotgun victim was hit at point-blank range on the right side of the head as confirmed from the hospital report. The Turkish boy who remembered this life was born with a malformed ear and an underdevelopment of the right side of his face.

One woman had three linear scar-like birthmarks on her back. As a child, she remembered being killed by three blows to her back with an ax. Another boy in India was born with stubs for fingers on only his right hand—an extremely rare condition. He remembered a past life when his fingers were cut off in a fodder chopping machine. (27)

Regarding the huge amount of evidence about birth marks and birth defects correlating with alleged present and past lives of the same person, Stevenson states, "I accept reincarnation as the best explanation for a case only after I have excluded all others—normal and paranormal. . . I regard my contribution as that of presenting the evidence as clearly as I can. Each reader should study the evidence carefully—preferably in the monograph (*Reincarnation and Biology*)—and then reach his or her own conclusion." (28)

Conclusions and Action Steps

This huge amount of varied evidence for reincarnation, a continuous but cyclical life process, is another important indication of afterlife for all and our eternal soul natures. Of particular note are the many subcategories of evidence that were just briefly covered in this chapter. Readers are encouraged to read widely from among the reference texts mentioned and, as Dr. Stevenson suggests, draw their own conclusions based on the existing evidence.

Suggested action steps include:

∞ Discuss these topics with loved ones, your minister, and church or spiritual support group

∞ Read further about this topic from among the texts quoted

∞ Reflect on how the idea of reincarnation fits with your belief system

∞ Experience a past life regression from a certified therapist; contact Dr. Weiss' organization (www.brianweiss.com) for specially trained therapists in your area

Benefit 8

**Having resolute knowledge that living—and dying—
are totally safe, fair, and purposeful**

I recently conducted a survey about the most pressing questions about religion and spirituality. Among the hundreds of responses were many "why" questions: "Why would God let anyone burn in hell forever? Why did God take my little child? Why does God allow so much injustice on earth? Why do angels help in some cases but not all? Why can't I know what my mission in life is? Why do I feel so confused and hopeless about helping others?"

These were not just abstract questions or mere intellectual curiosity. Each response contained heart-rending details that reflected immense suffering and struggle.

I'll come back to these excellent questions, but first, I have a question for you.

What if there was a sign by a roller coaster ride: "Everyone who rides on this will die. In addition, most of you will also burn afterwards in a fiery hell forever."

Would you want to go on such a ride? Of course not. Yet, ridiculous as it sounds, this represents a common teaching about what a Creator of unfathomable wisdom and love plans for us. No wonder so many people are confused about or want nothing to do with religion and spirituality. No wonder so many are ridden with fear, guilt, and disempowerment.

On the other hand, what if the sign said: "Everyone who rides on this rollercoaster will come through it completely safe and secure. There will, however, be some thrills and chills along the way. It may be a little scary at times as you go through the ups and downs along the tracks. You might even feel confused during the loops and temporarily lose your orientation about which is up and down. But don't worry. All of you will arrive safely and be much more courageous and wise for the experience."

The latter description is a fairly accurate one for this roller coaster ride we call life on planet earth. In fact, it's a beautiful analogy for the enlightened perspective that emerges when we realize the underlying spiritual reality—the unseen energetic matrix—that is the foundation of all life.

Now back to the questions. Based on the nine categories of evidence, much light is shed on these justifiable beefs.

1. "Why would God let anyone burn in hell forever?"

First, as discussed in the Religion and Spirituality Input chapter, much evidence indicates there is no fiery eternal hell.

Regarding why God would allow this or that, the more we personify God, the less accurately we perceive the Divine. The questions above assume a controlling Ruler that decides minute details about every aspect of life.

I don't see God that way at all. The Power and Presence described in the collective evidence is all pervading, everywhere, always. But He/She/It isn't a puppet master that constantly pulls strings affecting our lives: "This one dies, this one has to come back, I'll allow this suffering but not that one" and so on.

2. "Why did God take my little child?

Same answer about the nature of God. As for children passing on, we've already discussed the proof that even little children are immortal beings of energy. Maybe they didn't have to stay on earth for long before their missions were accomplished. Earth is only our temporary home. The physical passing of a child is horribly painful and seems unbearably tragic—I'm not minimizing that. From a spiritual perspective, though, it's a happy day when a soul graduates and gets to return Home—even when that soul inhabited the body of a young one.

3. "Why does God allow so much injustice on earth?"

Same answer about the nature of God. The injustices only seem that way when we look at a very small sliver of life instead of the entire pie. Eternity is a very long time and justice is surely served even though it doesn't seem that way in this short lifetime. The principles of karma and "an eye for an eye" reflect the way the universe works. We reap what we sow, inexorably. The model of reincarnation sheds much light on this subject.

4. "Why do God and the Heavenly Host (angels, guides, and spiritual masters) help in some cases but not all?"

My understandings about this excellent question include:

♦ They do not impose their will on others. If people make decisions to hurt themselves, that's their free will.

♦ We first need to ask for assistance, and then realize it may not always arrive how, when, and where we expect it.

♦ We will never know how often we are helped. Assistance may be subtle, undetectable, and preventive.

♦ Souls may have chosen significant challenges to assist spiritual growth and Creator/angels wouldn't interfere with this plan.

♦ Earth is designed to be a place of learning. If God and the Heavenly Host intervened and prevented all suffering, much of the earthly curriculum would be omitted.

5. "Why can't I know what my mission in life is?"

6. "Why do I feel so confused and hopeless about helping others?"

These are essentially the same question. Remember the first roller-coaster sign? Feeling confused and disempowered is a predictable consequence of believing this way.

So the first key is to prayerfully examine your heart and decide for yourself what makes sense. There are many different religious doctrines about the nature of God, salvation, and afterlife. They can't all be right. Given the available evidence, what feels most true to you?

Enjoying a personal relationship with Spirit in an atmosphere of safety and trust is a prerequisite for clearly knowing your life purpose.

See Benefit # 4 for a further discussion of how to identify your soul's purpose and how you can best serve others and God.

Knowing that living and dying are completely safe, fair, and purposeful allows us to face each day—no matter what our outer circumstances—with trust, faith, and clarity.

As you go through the ups and downs in life, remember the roller coaster metaphor and that life is a magnificent adventure with a happy ending—even when it doesn't seem like it.

Firsthand Experience & Other Ways Of Knowing

At age eleven, I sat with my family during church service. That particular morning, the minister mentioned hell in the context of a fiery eternal place of torment. As he continued, a loving and wise thought or voice resounded within and—it seemed at the time—all around me: "Mark, they are confused. God has no need for such a place in His plan of salvation for all."

Looking around to see if anyone else had heard this voice, I noticed that my family and other members of the congregation continued to stare straight ahead. Not wanting to seem kooky, I said nothing about what had happened, but life felt noticeably different after that. For the first time, I considered the possibility that ministers were merely passing on what they had learned in their training. I realized they were just people like me and they might be wrong about hell and about other things, too. That was my introduction to the concept of trusting my inner knowing.

For many, firsthand experience and inner knowing constitute the most incontrovertible proof of our eternal soul natures. Skeptics, atheists and scientific materialists can't dissuade those who have glimpsed their essential oneness with Spirit. As such, despite its subjectivity, this is one of the most personally convincing categories of evidence.

As Emanuel Swedenborg stated, "Do not believe me simply because I have seen heaven and hell, have discoursed with angels. . . Believe me because I tell you what your consciousness and intuitions will tell you if you listen closely to their voice." (1)

People are increasingly using intuition and subtle discernment to detect the breadth of reality that is generally not sensed. Our vocabulary reflects these other ways of perceiving nonphysical phenomena: gut feeling, inner voice, heartfelt emotions, second sight, and the mind's eye. Jesus spoke of hearing with ears that really hear and seeing with eyes that really see. The *nonsensate world*—that huge portion of reality that usually cannot be detected by the five senses —can be experienced in other ways.

Childhood Knowing

Some children vividly recall their spiritual essence. As soon as they can communicate—usually around age three—these little ones report remembering pre-earthly realms or seeing denizens of spirit world. For example, recall my comment as a five year old to my parents that a beautiful sunset reminded me of God. They couldn't think of any reason why I would associate the two; perhaps I remembered the Light from which I had recently arrived.

Another personal experience happened with our younger daughter when she was four years old. After her mother and I read her a bedtime story, she drifted off to sleep and murmured: "I remember before I came to be with you. The sun always shined, it never rained, and I always wore pretty dresses. And, oh yes, Greg was there too!" (Greg was a pre-school buddy with whom there was an immediate and strong mutual attraction.) Then she stopped talking. We waited, then quietly prompted her by asking, "Tell us more, what else do you remember?"

Our questions awakened her and she said, "Oh, I must have been dreaming."

In Western cultures, such reports often aren't taken seriously or, worse, they are ridiculed or punished. Around age five or six, children typically become more indoctrinated into the physical world and lose touch with unseen realities. This may occur for several reasons.

The souls of young children have just recently left spirit side, thus their remembrance of "the really real place" and detection of spirit beings. As discussed, overly active brain function can mask more subtle realities, but the cerebral cortexes of little ones aren't yet extensively utilized. It's probably no coincidence that most children lose their spiritual awareness when formal schooling begins. The new information, activities, and desire to "fit in" likely block or override more celestial perceptions.

I asked Dr. Wayne Dyer when he first glimpsed that he was a soul. He answered: "I think I've known that since I was able to talk and think. Even as a little boy, I knew there was much more. I knew how to not be in pain, I knew how to cultivate the witness. It's almost like leaving your body, you get in back of it and just watch it. I spent ten years in an orphanage and at times it was lonely and sad. I was able to step back and become the observer rather than what I observed. I think that's a big part of higher awareness, of soul consciousness." (2)

Significant evidence across time and cultures indicates the presence of spirit beings. Inhabitants of unseen dimensions—angels, spirit guides, whatever you call them—seem to exist and are sometimes detected by children. Perhaps it's time to give more credence to 'imaginary playmates' of children and encourage, rather than scorn, their otherworldly visions and memories. When broached sensitively, these topics won't confuse or upset children, but will reassure them that their perceptions may well be accurate.

Glimpsing Unity Consciousness

Personal experience provides glimpses of *unity* consciousness, an apprehension of the truth that we each are one with all life. Core beliefs of all religions maintain that deeply encountering our unity with the Ground of All Being is a potential for all people. Humans are, by nature, self-aware creatures who eventually gravitate toward realizing this unitive knowledge.

The highest level of human consciousness, unity or cosmic consciousness, is the awareness that none of us are separate from each other, that we are all connected. As the poet Rumi said, "I, you, me, he, she, they; these are distinctions which do not exist in the garden of the mystic."

In *No Boundary: Eastern and Western Approaches to Personal Growth*, Ken Wilber stated: "Unity consciousness is not a particular experience among other experiences, not a big experience opposed to small experiences. . . Rather, it is every wave of present experience just as it is . . . the true sages proclaim there is no path to the Absolute, no way to *gain* unity consciousness . . . there are *no means* to the ultimate, no techniques, no paths, and this is only because it is its nature to be omnipresent, present everywhere and everywhen . . . it is *this present experience* which always holds the key to our search." (3)

While driving over a long bridge recently, I enjoyed a cherished moment of oneness. Glancing up, I saw a flock of geese flying in front of a fading sunset. Then I looked over to see the river and its snowy banks. The entire scene seemed so familiar, as if I had helped design the entire vista. I felt an overwhelmingly deep sense of peace and oneness with all of life.

Haven't we each had at least one such moment? These sacred glimpses remind us there is a rhyme and a reason to all seasons of life. Fleeting peeks can evolve into fuller perceptions of absolute reality that death does not exist and suffering is optional. Our real selves *are inextricably intertwined* with Unity Consciousness now. Our inner beings are inseparably and eternally one with the Ground of All Being. Enlightenment, then, is not a matter of achieving but remembering.

John 17:21 reflects this theme of unity consciousness, of realizing we each are one with God. This passage says that Jesus prayed, ". . . that they all may be One; as thou, Father, art in me, and I in thee, that they also may be One in us. . ." The same sense is echoed in other religions, for example, 'All is Allah' in Islam, 'I am That' in Hinduism, and 'Hear, O' Israel, the Lord thy God is One' in Judaism. The *Bhagavad-Gita* states, "They live in wisdom who see themselves in all and all in them."

Realizing we are part and parcel of this unitive consciousness makes any questions about afterlife nonsensical. From this vantage point, our real selves are always securely planted in eternity. Each soul is like a drop of water and God is like the ocean. As such, we each are important and integral parts of that phenomenon. As the *Upanishads* state, "The shining Self dwells hidden in the heart. Everything in the cosmos, great and small, lives in the Self. He is the source of life, truth beyond the transience of this world." (4)

Awareness of our interconnectedness with all life reminds us of our inner being that transcends time and space. The key is to avoid excessive identification with the physical body and ego-based personality that change when we drop the body. As the *Bhagavad-*

Gita teaches: "The all-knowing Self was never born, nor will it die. Beyond cause and effect, this Self is eternal and immutable. When the body dies, the Self does not die. If the slayer believes that he can slay or the slain believes that he can be slain, neither knows the truth." (5)

Once you behold this reality, even in a fragmented or momentary way, life is never the same. You then wonder how this good news wasn't apparent before since all life shouts it.

You've no doubt seen drawings that contain two or more pictures. Some people can see only one picture whereas others readily see the other perspectives. Similarly, certain people have blinders that keep them from comprehending spiritual insights more fully. These include restrictive social conditioning, religious training, and lack of exposure or openness to new information.

There are numerous ways to first glimpse and eventually internalize unity consciousness. These techniques are collectively known as *centering practices.*

Centering Practices

William Blake said, "If the doors of perception were cleansed, everything would appear to man as it is, infinite." *Meditation and prayer* are paramount for clearer perception, for firsthand awareness of spiritual realities. Paramahansa Yogananda said, "Why should you think He is not everywhere? The air is filled with music that is caught by the radio—music that otherwise you would not know about. And so it is with God. He is with you every minute of your existence, yet the only way to realize this is to meditate." Of the importance of daily quieting the mind, Father Thomas Keating says: "Silence is the language God speaks, and everything else is a bad translation."

Other *centering practices* include: yoga, service to others, time with loved ones, gardening, chanting, breathing exercises, drumming, playing with pets, time with elders, sewing, spiritual study, exercising, spinning, bodywork, energy movement practices like tai chi and qi gong, experiential seminars, hot baths, enlightened lovemaking, psycho-spiritual work, deep relaxation, shamanic drumming and trance work, and spiritual dance. These activities temporarily turn down the brain's chatter and help us realize how safely we each are embedded in eternity. They allow access to time-less moments in which we recall our oneness with Universe.

Regarding the importance of centering practices, Houston Smith, Ph.D., stated: "The senses turn inward. As bridges to the physical world they are invaluable, but the *yogi* is seeking something else. On the track of more interesting prey—the interior universe in which (according to reports) is to be found the final secret of life's mystery—the *yogi* wants no sense bombardments. . . . For the *yogi* is tracking the underpinning of life's façade. Behind its physical front, where we experience the play of life and death, the *yogi* seeks a deeper life that knows no death." (6)

The great Indian saint Sri Ramakrishna was asked: "Do you believe in God, sir?" "Yes," he replied. "Can you prove it, sir?" "Yes." "How?" "Because I see Him just as I see you here, only more intensely." I had a very intense multi-sensory experience of the Source in 1997 during a long yoga and meditation session.

While silently repeating the mantra OM, a louder and deeper chorus of that sound spontaneously resounded within and all around me. I smelled an unknown but wonderful fragrance although the windows and doors were shut. Even though my eyes were shut, I saw a radiant golden-white light in my mind's eye. Then I felt what seemed to be Divine love, acceptance, and understanding. This peek of the Beloved was so overwhelmingly beautiful that tears welled up in my eyes.

It seemed that information and energy were being transmitted to me. The power and splendor were so great that, after just a few minutes, I felt I couldn't handle the current. I murmured aloud, "Oh my God!" and started laughing, and then the glimpse was over. But that sweet memory helps carry me through life's challenges and reminds me I'm always Home, no matter what the external circumstances.

One teaching from that event is that I was not prepared to directly experience Divine frequencies for very long. That level of power blew my mind's circuit breakers; my nervous system wasn't strong enough to handle the current. This experience motivates me to live as healthy and godly a life as possible so I can increasingly sustain that energy level.

That's the main reason for practicing centering techniques: not to work oneself toward God—She is always present and available.

Such methods help upgrade the power and purity of our perception so we can comprehend reality more accurately. Energy, love, light, intelligence, and joy are the totality of life. All else is an illusion. Certain holistic techniques and understandings help us remember and experience that truth firsthand.

Breathwork is an ancient and cross-cultural way to encounter our eternal natures firsthand. In the Aramaic and Hebrew languages, the words *spirit* and *breath* were used interchangeably. The Chinese word *chi* and Japanese *ki* variously mean life force, spirit, and breath. Breathing techniques are simple and powerful, but still relatively unknown.

Many amazing benefits have occurred as I've facilitated many group breathwork sessions over the years. For example, a sixty year-old female cried and cried for fifteen minutes while rolled up in a fetal position. She then became very still and quiet for the rest of the session. Afterwards, I asked what she experienced. During the quiet time, she visited departed loved ones—her husband, parents, and several pets that had passed on. She emphatically stated, "I'm totally convinced I was really visiting with them in another dimension; it wasn't just my imagination or a visualization."

A number of breathwork participants have also reported experiencing visits to *spiritual realms* during their sessions. These reports were quite similar to those of NDEs with perceptions of beings of light, profound peace, being embraced by the Light, and a reluctance to return to waking consciousness. Some experienced energetic healing while others felt that important information was being received.

The spiritually transformational impact of breathwork was perhaps best described by a seventy year-old woman in South Carolina whose forty-five year-old daughter had recently passed over. After tearfully letting go of much pain and sadness, she felt certain her daughter was an older soul that didn't need a long life to achieve its objectives. This woman felt a newfound peace and acceptance about her daughter's passing. "I used to think I was here to teach her," she shared, "but now I know she was here to teach me."

Perhaps you've seen Oriental art depicting a wise sage standing on a bridge, impassively watching the river flow below. Regular prayer, meditation, and other centering techniques enable a firsthand experience of the richness of life. From this 'watcher state,' we can calmly yet passionately participate in all life's changes while deeply knowing that life never ends.

Consider the following quotes that point to the importance of centering practices:

- Pascal: "All man's miseries derive from not being able to sit quietly in a room alone."

- Pythagoras: "Learn to be silent. Let your quiet mind listen and absorb."

- John Donne: "Wilt thou love God, as he Thee? Then digest, My Soul, this wholesome meditation: How God, the Spirit, by Angels waited on in Heaven, doth make his Temple in thy brest."

- Rumi, the thirteenth-century Sufi mystic: "Secretly we spoke, that wise one and me. I said, 'Tell me the secrets of the world.' He said, 'Ssssh, let silence tell you the secrets of the world.'"

Common Sense

Eternity for all is the simplest explanation given life's apparent inequalities. If there is just this lifetime, it doesn't seem fair: some people are healthy, attractive and born into educated, loving families whereas others experience just the opposite. The playing field is leveled if we each indeed are eternal souls. There *is* justice in the Universe when seen with a spiritual perspective.

That we all continue on after physical death just makes sense. This was beautifully stated in *Go Toward The Light* by Chris Oyler who described the moments after her nine year-old son passed on after contracting AIDS from a blood transfusion: "The room was full of Ben. He was all around us everywhere. Warm and loving. He was lingering for a moment to say good-by. To tell us not to worry, that there wasn't anything to be afraid of, and never was... And you know that all that energy and love cannot just vanish without a trace." (7)

The "Swiss watch" analogy is one common sense argument for the existence of a wise Higher Power and, thus, a good and just outcome for all creation. Following the logic of this "intelligent design" philosophy, imagine that you were walking down the street and found an expensive Swiss watch on the ground. Would you conclude that the watch just fell out of the sky and existed as the result of random luck? Or might you suspect that an organizing intelligence, like a fine watch maker, created the watch and someone lost it?

In the same way, consider the awesome complexity and intelligence—evident on both the macro and micro levels—in the human body, nature, and universe. An equally awesome Creative Force is implied. Wouldn't you think such Infinite Intelligence has an equally wise and just plan for all people?

Paramahansa Yogananda wrote, "Death gives new roles to actor-souls so that they may play in new dramas on the stage of life." What a concise and reasonable explanation for why there is death and change! Imagine how bored you would become watching the same movie over and over again. You wouldn't learn anything new and you wouldn't be entertained. Life is the same way even though we sometimes wish we could freeze time and suspend change. A constant sameness would preclude new opportunities for growth and service that led us to choose this earthly classroom in the first place.

Some spiritual teachers say there are no accidents, that there is an exquisitely perfect Divine design. I can believe this for the most part, but it's more difficult to accept when children pass on or when mass deaths occur as in the Holocaust. Events such as these really test our faith and make it more difficult to see through the illusion that physicality is all there is.

When I asked Wayne Dyer about the concept that there are no accidents or tragedies, he replied:

It's only a tragedy if you believe that dying is a tragedy. It's not if you understand that everyone comes in and leaves when they're supposed to. Our egos and our ideologies say that children shouldn't die and that no one should leave until they are one hundred and six years-old and pass away in their sleep at night. But that's not the way the universe works. We show up here for the amount of time we're supposed to be here.

This is an intelligent system that we're all part of. Just imagine this for a moment: let's say you've got a junkyard with about ten million parts. There are toilet seats, broken glass, wires, pipes and all kinds of upholstery, screws, nuts, and bolts and so on. All of a sudden, a big wind comes through and starts blowing all of these parts around. They blow up into a cyclone and then the wind passes. You look at the field where that junk yard was and sitting there is a Boeing 747, all ready to fly you off to London. What are the chances of something like that happening? Pretty slim.

Well, that's the same chance that our world just happened by accident. And there aren't just 10 million parts but zillions upon zillions of interwoven parts, all fitting together perfectly—not just on our planet but in billions and billions of other galaxies. The assumption behind the notion that this is all just an accident—that there is no force or intelligence behind it—is just as foolish and arrogant as assuming a windstorm could blow together ten million parts and create a 747. There's an intelligence behind everything in the universe and therefore there are no accidents in it. (8)

I know this is difficult to fathom, especially if you are now dying or actively grieving the passing of a loved one or broken relationship. Eternity is a long time and there will be ample opportunities to be with loved ones again. From this timeless perspective, consider the possibility that there is a rhythm and timing to all events. One key to having a breakthrough into awakening is to have faith, not fear.

Living with Faith

Fear is a major obstacle that keeps people from enjoying a firsthand awareness of spiritual realities. Rev. Norman Vincent Peale said, "Fear knocked on my door. Faith answered. No one was there." *A Course in Miracles* teaches, "If you knew Who walks beside you on the way that you have chosen, fear would be impossible."

Regarding the Buddha, Huston Smith, Ph.D., states, "In his later years, when India was afire with his message and kings themselves were bowing before him, people came to him even as they were to come to Jesus asking what he was. . . . the answer he gave provided an identity for his entire message. 'Are you a god?' they asked. 'No.' 'An angel?' 'No.' 'A saint?' 'No.' 'Then what are you?' Buddha answered, 'I am awake.'" (9)

To become awakened requires seeing through the illusions perpetuated by fear. As a multitude of evidence indicates, we each really are timeless spiritual beings. Death is just a transition so the soul can move on to new adventures and callings. The more we awaken, the more we can live with faith, hope, and courage—not fear.

Spending time with dying people is an excellent way to work through fears about life's greatest transition. I've been with many hundreds of people as they died so death is not a stranger or a fearful unknown. Most people have a wonderfully peaceful look on their face just before and/or after dropping the body. Being present during just one graduation to another realm is a special gift that reduces fear.

Emily Dickinson wrote, "Because I could not stop for death, he kindly stopped for me. The carriage held but just ourselves. And immortality." White Eagle stated, "You live on earth only for a few short years which you call an incarnation, and then you leave your body as an outworn dress and go for refreshment to your true Home in the spirit." Notice their words 'kindly' and 'go for refreshment'? These are much more apt images of death than that of a grim reaper.

In *The Little Prince*, Antoine De Saint-Exupery stated: "It is only with the heart that one can see rightly; what is essential is invisible to the eye." When we perceive reality clearly, without the interference of fear, we realize and accept the impermanence of this world. We see through the illusion that the physical is all there is. As Buddha said, "Regard this phantom world as a star at dawn, a bubble in a stream, a flash of lightning in a summer cloud, a flickering lamp—a phantom—and a dream." (10)

Trusting, not fearing, our innermost feeling assists a greater inner knowing. Regarding the question of whether individual mystical experiences furnish any proof for the truth of immortality, William James replied, "Mystical states, when well developed, usually are, and have the right to be, absolutely authoritative over the individuals to whom they come. . . . They break down the authority of the non-mystical or rationalistic consciousness, based upon the understanding and the senses alone. They show it to be only one kind of consciousness. They open out the possibility of other orders of truth, in which, so far as anything in us vitally responds to them, we may freely continue to have faith." (11)

Dr. Dyer says, "Everything you see, everything you experience with your senses, will someday be 'quiet dust.' Yet the part of you that is noticing all this is never the 'quiet dust.' . . . everything and everyone has a circuit to fulfill, and when it is complete, it ceases in its current form and shifts to another. The material of our bodies is recycled, while our true essence remains . . . This awareness is a great source of liberation; it is your ticket to eternity. It allows you to stop fearing death." (12)

That's when life really begins. As Kahlil Gibran said, "When the earth shall claim your limbs, then shall you truly dance." But we don't have to wait until we die to experience unitive consciousness and heaven on earth. We each can enjoy vibrant awareness whenever we know—through faith and knowledge—that our bodies will die someday, but our real selves are timeless.

First-Hand Experiences

Incredible firsthand experiences have been reported by respected people from all walks of life.

An experience at a holistic health retreat in 1996 further convinced me of the reality of spirit world. I was walking toward the ocean and clearly saw two people swimming and standing in the water. As I waded in, I saw a tall male with dark hair and a shorter female bobbing and diving under the water. As I approached even closer, the female waved at me and I recognized her as my good friend Elaine.

I wondered who the man was since her husband was shorter and had white hair. I couldn't see him and figured he was holding his breath under water. When I reached Elaine, I looked all around and asked, "Where's that guy?" She looked at me like I was crazy and said, "What guy? I've been out here by myself for twenty minutes." I described the fellow I had seen as clearly as I had seen her. "Maybe you saw my spirit guide," she said. Maybe.

Having contact with non-physical beings is not so strange. The esteemed Dr. Wayne Dyer states, "I have had messages from another world although I don't think of it as another world, it's all one world. When it was time for me to leave drinking and drugs behind in my life, I received a very strong message in the middle of the night. I heard, absolutely heard, a voice that said: 'I will guide you through this. You will never struggle with this again.' And I walked away from those addictions." (13)

Most impressively, many thousands of people have been healed by prayer, faith healing, and Higher Power based twelve step programs like AA, AlAnon, ACOA, and OA. Research has shown that the person in need doesn't even have to know about the prayers to receive a cure. These miraculous cures are powerful firsthand experiences that suggest unseen forces at work.

Entheogens are plants and chemical substances that awaken or generate firsthand mystical experiences. With the same root word as enthusiasm, entheogens refer to *bringing God within*. I can't recommend this approach for most people because of the potential pitfalls: misuse, addiction, and related illnesses or accidents.

However, I recognize that numerous people have had their spiritual eyes opened via use of certain mind altering plants. Religious and mystical practices in various cultures have gainfully used sacred botanical preparations to heighten awareness. However, because of legalities and safety issues, I prefer and recommend the centering practices listed above as optimal routes to nonordinary states of consciousness.

Interested readers can learn more about the entheogen path to spiritual awakening by reading selected books by Ram Dass (aka Richard Alpert, Ph.D.), Fred Alan Wolfe, Ph.D., Carlos Castaneda, Ph.D., Stan Grof, M.D., and Dennis McKenna, Ph.D.

Finally, let us remember the tremendous power of realizing that the kingdom of heaven is at hand. In the *Lord's Prayer*, we pray: "Thy kingdom come, on earth as it is in heaven." That can happen with each one of us today. Taking time to experience this reality firsthand yields magnificent benefits.

The Arts and Consciousness

Another way of glimpsing the reality of Spirit firsthand is through *the arts*. In *The Care of the Soul*, Thomas Moore, Ph.D., states:

> Arts, broadly speaking, is that which invites us into contemplation—a rare commodity in modern life. In that moment of contemplation, art intensifies the presence of the

world. We see it more vividly and more deeply. The emptiness that many people complain dominates their lives comes in part from a failure to let the world in, to perceive it and engage it fully.

> Children paint every day and love to show their works on walls and refrigerator doors. But as we become adults, we abandon this important soul task of childhood. . . . maybe they are learning something more fundamental: finding forms that reflect what is going on in their souls. Art captures the eternal in the everyday, and it is the eternal that feeds the soul—the whole world in a grain of sand. (14)

Many creative people have been inspired to express their glimpses of the Divine in various forms. Emanuel Swedenborg's writings and William Blake's engravings are two examples of capturing visions in art form. The famous angel artist Andy Lakey was inspired to paint after his spiritual conversion from being a drug addict. His paintings have assisted thousands of people to have healings and revelations.

One painting from the 15th century depicted a scene commonly described in near-death experiences —a darkened tunnel with bright light at the end and various angels and otherworldly citizens hovering about. Numerous artists have captured other beautiful renditions of angels and light beings. These include: Gustave Dore, Matthias Grunewald, Botticelli, Blake, Pieta, Rembrandt, and da Vinci. Sculptors from antiquity have memorialized angels in their work, some of which survives to this day. Inspiring movies and theatrical productions also nourish the human spirit with a rich blend of music, dance, theme, and acting.

Music can also serve as a vehicle to connecting with our immortal selves. Great music inspires our souls and reminds us of loftier realms and our highest potentials. Certain chords touch our emotions deeply and instantaneously. A tuning fork-like effect creates concordant vibrations, a cascade of wavelengths between the musical notes and our inner emotions. Certain classical and New Age music may remind us of celestial sounds from the other side and thus trigger recall of our timeless nature.

In her book *Interior Castle*, Teresa of Avila discussed the concept of various rooms in the mansion of the soul: ". . . your soul has millions of rooms, most of which never have their doors opened.

And in every one of them there are labyrinths and fountains and jewels and gems and gardens." Matthew Fox comments, "I just love that. I remember once I was lying on my living room floor listening to opera and in the middle I said, 'Why am I listening to opera, who needs opera?' Then that line from Teresa of Avila came through— we have to open up these doors of the soul, and maybe even opera can do this. Why die before we've opened at least a million doors!" (15)

Great *writers* throughout the ages have described their conviction about the reality of eternity:

♦ John Greenleaf Whittier: "A presence strange at once and known, walked with me as my life guide; the skirts of some forgotten life, trailed noiselessly at my side."

♦ Louisa May Alcott: "I seem to remember former states and feel that in them I have learned some of the lessons that have never since been mine here, and in my next step I hope to leave behind many of the trials I have struggled to bear here and begin to find lightened as I go on."

♦ Ralph Waldo Emerson: "Great men are they who see that spiritual is stronger than any material force, that thoughts rule the world."

♦ Helen Keller: "Death . . . is no more than passing from one room into another. But there's a difference for me, you know. Because in that other room I shall be able to see again."

♦ Herman Melville: "Methinks we have hugely mistaken this matter of Life and Death. . . . Methinks my body is but the least of my better body. In fact take my body who will, take it I say, it is not me."

♦ John Milton: "Millions of spiritual creatures walk the earth unseen, both when we wake and when we sleep. What if earth and heaven be to each other like more than on earth is thought?"

♦ Goethe: "The thought of death leaves me in perfect peace, for I have a firm conviction that our spirit is a being of indestructible nature."

♦ William Wordsworth: "Our birth is but a sleep and forgetting; the Soul that rises with us, our life's star, hath had elsewhere its setting, and cometh from afar: not in entire forgetfulness, and not in utter nakedness, but trailing clouds of glory do we come from God, who is our Home."

Perhaps the contributions of artists, musicians and writers are so deeply felt because, ultimately, many aspects of the soul are ineffable. Matters of another dimension can't be adequately described in words. As soon as we try to name or define the Infinite in human terms, we have lost much of Its richness, mystery, and essence.

Conclusions and Action Steps

Centering practices, common sense, firsthand experience, and the arts remind us who we are, why we're here, and where we're going. These are ways, as Robert Browning put it, 'to open out a way' for our inner light to emerge. This challenging world makes more sense when we have firsthand experiences and really know—without a doubt—about our essential spiritual natures.

Action steps for this category might be:

∞ Reflect upon firsthand experiences you have had and review the lessons from them

∞ Meditate and pray on a regular basis to quiet the mind and hear Spirit

∞ Consider other centering practices such as yoga, breathwork, and nature walks

∞ Enjoy great arts to better appreciate the miracles that abound within and all around us

Benefit 9

Excitement about a joyful eternity of loving, learning, enjoying, and serving

Question: With a center shot from ten feet away, which of the following weapons would kill your soul *the most*?

a. a BB gun

b. a .358 magnum pistol

c. a bazooka

d. a nuclear missile

The answer is two paragraphs below. Please answer the question before reading further.

French philosopher Voltaire said that God is like a comedian playing to an audience that's afraid to laugh. You've probably seen slapstick comedy where someone died very dramatically, pumped his feet up in the air, had many 'last words', kicked the bucket, and other humorous stunts. Just imagine how funny all our grief about death is since we merely enter a different room in Creator's mansion.

Life is an infinite journey with endless opportunities for loving, adventure, enjoyment, and service to others. The same energy and intelligence that created and sustains the universe also resides within each one of us. The more we fathom this, the more we realize how exciting and awesome life is in every way.

Oh, by the way, the answer to the quiz is: None of the above. Your real self—spirit, soul, consciousness, awareness—can't be killed by anything.

Sorry for the trick question, but I wanted to test how much you really get this. Realizing we are forever beings helps us celebrate the good news that we are already firmly planted amidst eternity. Eternity doesn't start someday, maybe. It's happening now. This is it. That awakening helps us go through life with an attitude of trust, confidence, and excitement. Even through 'bad' or difficult events.

Helen Keller said that life is either a daring adventure or it is nothing at all. Many of us lead 'lives of quiet desperation' and try to just cope from one difficulty to another. I've certainly done my share of this and am not criticizing those who are still overly immersed in the melodrama. But, again, consider how ludicrous all our suffering is when we're merely acting out one of an infinite numbers of plays. Life *is* a daring adventure. We can best realize that and live accordingly when we know—without a doubt—that we are soul proof.

Just think how immeasurably better life will be as we see Spirit at work in every life situation. For example:

♦ When a loved one passes on, saying and knowing: "She graduated to a higher plane. When I cross over someday, she'll be there to greet me!"

♦ When a relationship breaks up: "Our time together has come to an end for now, but eternity is a long time and I'm sure we'll cross paths again!"

♦ When financial loss occurs: "Although I wouldn't have chosen this, it will take me down different roads in life and create new opportunities for growing, experiencing, and serving!"

Likewise for all the other challenges of life. When viewed through spiritual eyes, there is no 'misfortune', it's just life unfolding with its perpetual change and endless experiences. If Helen Keller can see life as an exciting adventure, we all can.

Much evidence indicates that our souls choose certain life circumstances for the growth and service opportunities therein. From a spiritual perspective, we know that it's worth it to go through tribulation for a relatively short time.

Viktor E. Frankl, M.D., Ph.D., survivor of Nazi death camps and author of *Man's Search for Meaning*, termed this enhanced perspective as *supra-meaning*. He asked whether an ape used in research to develop polio serum would grasp the meaning of its suffering. Only from a human perspective could the ape understand why it was repeatedly punctured for blood samples.

Then Frankl asks, "And what about man? Are you sure that the human world is a terminal point in the evolution of the cosmos? Is it not conceivable that there is still another dimension possible, a world beyond man's world; a world in which the question of an ultimate meaning of human suffering would find an answer?" (16)

During a spiritual regression, one woman recalled a past life and the subsequent time in spirit world. During the earthly life, she was plagued by one disappointment after another. Her life seemed to be a series of failures, broken dreams, sadness, and loneliness. However, when she passed on, she found that these hardships had prepared her for a particularly demanding role on the other side: helping heal recently departed souls who had been abused to death as babies. Her earthly struggles had strengthened her spirit and deepened her compassion sufficiently to serve in that demanding way. So, you tell me, was her earthly suffering worth it?

In my work with many thousands of people in hospitals, mental health centers, private practice, and workshops, I've witnessed amazing personal transformations. I've seen hardened people—whose hearts I thought would never open in this lifetime—change into loving, angelic-like beings as a result of suffering. This strengthens my belief that life makes perfect sense when we remember that it's exquisitely designed for optimal spiritual growth.

One example is "Harold", a bear of a man who suffered with severe emphysema after many years of smoking. He was very demanding and belligerent during his increasingly frequent hospitalizations and most staff disliked working with him. Over a two-year period, however, I noticed him slowly but surely changing. At first, saying "thank you" and making small signs of civility. Then opening up and sharing how difficult it was to miss out on activities he loved like fishing and hunting. And breathing.

Later, as his condition worsened, he cried and apologized for what a mean SOB he used to be. Finally, as he fought for each breath, a peace and acceptance overcame him until he mercifully passed on. Although he suffered horribly, his transformation was marked and total. Toward the end, he was like an angel.

We don't have to suffer to grow spiritually. By all means, do everything you can to be totally successful: healthy, happy, prosperous, enjoying loving relationships and meaningful life work. But when life serves up a challenging curve ball, remember that it's all good. The blessing may not be obvious now, but it will be someday.

Humans are immortal souls having temporary earthly adventures. Being on this planet isn't easy, but it offers immense opportunities for soul growth, service to others, and enjoying a variety of experiences. When we remember that, no matter what our current circumstances, we can fully live each day with excitement, joy, and gratitude.

Afterword

"Let us live as if we were immortal." - Aristotle

I end this book the way I started: with Aristotle's statement. Over two thousand years ago, there was limited proof available. An immense amount of varied evidence now collectively proves that our spiritual selves are immortal even though our bodies are mortal.

A paradigm shift is occurring, a shift from viewing death as the end—or, even worse, a possible doorway into hell for eternity—to that of magnificently merging with an all-wise and loving Light. The evidence presented in *Soul Proof* helps us shift our views of death away from horrific images of the Grim Reaper. Instead, we can envision an infinitely loving and sustaining Divine Presence that exists within and all around us.

As you have seen, a huge amount of varied and validated evidence strongly indicates that we really are eternal souls. Much convincing proof indicates that—at our cores—we really are time-less spiritual beings, ever-changing but unending reflections of the Infinite Light. It's the way the Universe is set up.

I now return to my two questions in the introduction. First, after considering the evidence, are you more personally convinced about the reality of your indestructible spiritual nature and the existence of afterlife? Secondly, now that you have this knowledge, how will it shape the way you live, the way you treat others and yourself?

While starting to rouse from a deep sleep recently, I was aware that a phrase was repeating over and over in my mind. When I became sufficiently awake to engage my brain, I quickly wrote it down: 'Life is a totally safe and magnificent adventure amidst eternity.'

That's the bottom line, one that I hope you deeply understand and live by—now that you know your true nature.

Let's review the many benefits of a strong, internalized knowledge of your indestructible spiritual nature:

1. Experiencing little or no fear and grief about your own "death and dying" and that of your loved ones

2. Greater trust about all the rhythms of life, even those involving suffering and tragedy

3. A deeper understanding, or least peace, about life's existential questions: Who am I, why am I here, Is there a God, what happens when we die, and so on?

4. Increased clarity and courage to follow your purpose and heartfelt joys

5. More peace and acceptance about aging and bodily degeneration

6. Feeling closer to and grateful for God and the heavenly host

7. Appreciation for and optimal care of your soul's bodily temple

8. Resolute knowledge that living—and dying—are totally safe, fair, and purposeful

9. Excitement about a joyful eternity of loving, learning, enjoying, and serving

These benefits are enlightening, healing, and life transforming. Now it's time to live, love, enjoy, and serve others in the ways you feel called. As the old church hymn exhorts, "Brighten the corner where you are!" Now you can do so more radiantly.

May you always deeply know and vibrantly live your high soul nature. The evidence is clear: we each are immortal. Let us live accordingly!

Sharing More Evidence
and
Your Firsthand Experiences

There is, no doubt, much more evidence out there—just waiting to be documented and shared. Please bring any such information to my attention so that I may, in turn, tell others about additional proof of our true nature.

For many people, firsthand experiences are the most impressive evidence that we are immortal spirit beings. I welcome you to share any personal experiences, ADCs for example, that you and your loved ones have had. Please send these stories to the email or postal address below.

I will handle all contributions with complete confidentiality. If your story is used, I will change names and places for anonymity. Thank you in advance for sharing your firsthand factual stories that will further add to this impressive collection of evidence.

Mark Pitstick, MA, DC

mark@soulproof.com

Box 1604; Chillicothe, OH 45601

References

Introduction

1.) Webster's Third New International Dictionary. Chicago: William Benton, 1966.

2.) Oyler, Chris. *Go Toward The Light.* New York: Harper & Row, 1988. p. 60.

Evidence Category #1: After Death Contacts

1.) Moody, Raymond. *Reunions.* New York: Ivy Books, 1993. p. 16

2.) Ibid. p. 11.

3.) Peale, Norman Vincent. "The Glorious Message of Easter." *Plus—The Magazine of Positive Living.* Pawling, NY: Peale Center for Christian Living, March 1994.

4.) Jung, Carl. *Memories, Dreams, Reflections.* New York: Pantheon Books, 1973. p. 343-344.

5.) Guggenheim, Bill and Judy. *Hello from Heaven.* New York: Bantam Books, 1995. p. 283.

6.) Siegel, Bernie. *Love, Medicine, & Miracles.* New York: Harper & Row, 1986. p. 222-223.

7.) Moody, *Reunions*, p. 23

8.) Moody. *The Last Laugh.* Charlottesville, VA: Hampton Roads, 1999. p. 161.

9.) Moody, Raymond and Pitstick, Mark. *The Best of "Soul-utions".* Chillicothe, OH: Soul Proof Productions, 2000. (audiotapes and CDs of radio interviews)

10.) Reported in InfoBeat, May 1, 2001, regarding Paul McCartney's interview on ABC's *Good Morning America*

11.) Dass, Ram, and Gorman, Paul. *How Can I Help?* New York: Alfred Knopf, 1988. p. 85.

12.) Dyer and Pitstick, *The Best of "Soul-utions"*

13.) Newton, Michael. *Journey of Souls.* St. Paul, MN: Llewellyn, 1994. p. 219.

Evidence Category #2: Near-Death Experiences

1.) Moody, Raymond. *The Light Beyond.* Bantam: New York, 1988. p.104-105.

2.) Ring, Ken. *Lessons from the Light.* Portsmouth, NH: Moment Press, 1998. p. 56-58.

3.) Weiss, Brian. *Messages From The Masters.* New York: Warner Books, 2000. p. 168-171.

4.) Morse, Melvin and Perry, Paul. *Closer To The Light.* Ballantine: New York, 1990. p. 20.

5. Moody, *The Light Beyond*, p. 173.

6.) Morse, Melvin and Perry, Paul. *Transformed By The Light.* New York: Ivy Books, 1992. p. 123.

7.) Morse and Perry, *Closer To The Light*, p. 121, 4, 40-42.

8.) Moody, *The Light Beyond*, p. 28-29.

9.) Ring, *Lessons from the Light*, p. 151.

10.) Freeman, Sidney. *Life After Death.* Commack, NY: Kroshka Books, 1998. p. 79-80.

11.) personal communication with Joan Borysenko; story also told in *Fire In the Soul.* New York: Warner Books, 1993. p. 147.

12.) Moody, *The Last Laugh*, p. 4-5.

13.) Grof, Stanislav. *Books of the Dead.* London: Thames & Hudson, 1994. p. 31.

14.) Ring and Cooper, *Mindsight*. Palo Alto, CA: Wm. James Center for Consciousness Studies, 1999. p.xv.

15.) Ibid., p. 109-122.

16.) *U.S. News & World* Report; March 31, 1997.

17.) Moody, *The Light Beyond*, p.39-40.

18.) Ring, *Lessons from the Light*, p.163.

Evidence Category #3: Miraculous and Revelatory Experiences:

1.) Burnham, Sophy. *A Book of Angels.* New York: Ballantine Books, 1990. p. 26-27, 18-21.

2.) Spalding, Baird T. *Life and Teaching of the Masters of the Far East.* Marina del Rey, CA: DeVorss & Co, 1924.

3.) Morgan, Marlo. *Mutant Message Down Under.* New York: HarperCollins, 1991. p.93.

4.) Siegel, Bernie. *Love, Medicine & Miracles.* New York: Harper & Row, 1986. p. 219-220.

5.) Dyer, Wayne and Dyer, Marcelene. *A Promise Is A Promise.* Carlsbad, CA: Hay House, 1996. p. 75, 79-81, 28.

6.) Millman, Dan and Childers, Doug. *Divine Interventions.* Emmaus, PA: Rodale Books, 1999. p.193-196.

Evidence Category #4: Scientific Input

1.) Webster's Third New International Dictionary. Chicago: William Benton, 1966.

2.) Freeman, *Life After Death*, p. 215, 40-42.

3.) Fox, Matthew and Sheldrake, Rupert. *Natural Grace.* New York: Doubleday, 1996. p. 75-77.

4.) Mishlove and Pitstick, *The Best of "Soul-utions"*, 2000.

5.) Karger, Friedbert. From *Columbus (OH) Dispatch* article. October 8 1995.

6.) Penfield, Wilder. *The Mystery of the Mind.* Princeton, N.J.: Princeton University Press, 1975. p. 85.

7.) Wade, Jenny. *Changes Of Mind.* Albany, NY: State Univ. of NY Press, 1996. p. 2.

8.) Weiss, *Messages from the Masters*, p. 237.

9.) Morse, Melvin. From foreword to *The Other side and Back* by Sylvia Browne. New York: Signet, 2000. p. xi.

10.) Harmon, Willis. "The Re-emergence of the Survival Question." *Noetic Sciences Review*, Winter 1994, p. 30-33.

11.) Schwartz, Gary. *The Afterlife Experiments: Break-through Scientific Evidence Of Life After Death.* New York: Pocket Books, 2002. p. vii, xviii, xxii.

12.) Stevenson, Ian. W*here Reincarnation and Biology Intersect.* Westport, CT: Praeger Publishing, 1997. *p.*197.

13.) Freeman, *Life After Death.*, p. 227-228.

14.) Folger, Tim. Physics' Best Kept Secret. *Discover.* Sept. 2001: 36-43.

15.) Morse, (from foreword to) *The Other side and Back,* 2000.

16.) LeShan, Lawrence. *The Medium, the Mystic, and the Physicist.* New York: Viking Press, 1966. p. 258-259.

17.) Chopra, Deepak. *365 Days Of Love And Healing.* (calendar of sayings) Workman Publishing, 1996.

18.) James, William. *Varieties of Religious Experience.* New York: New American Library, 1958. p. 298.

19.) Russell, Peter. From keynote address at International Conference on Science and Consciousness. Albuquerque, NM. 1999.

20.) Becker, Robert. *The Body Electric.* New York: William Morrow, 1985. p. 21.

Evidence Category #5: Paranormal

1.) Martin, Joel and Romanowski, Patricia. *We Don't Die.* New York: Berkeley Books, 1988. p. 7, 110, 276-284.

2.) Weiss, *Messages From The Masters,* p.186-188.

3.) Schwartz and Simon, *The Afterlife Experiments,* p. 266, xviii, 222.

4.) Browne, Sylvia. *The Other side and Back.* New York: Signet, 2000. p.1-2.

5.) Martin, Joel and Romanowski, Patricia. *We Are Not Forgotten.* New York: Berkeley Books, 1991. p. 261-265.

6.) Van Praagh, James. *Talking to Heaven.* New York: Dutton, 1997. p.53-54.

7.) Altea, Rosemary. *The Eagle and The Rose.* New York: Warner, 1995. p. 111.

8.) Edward, John. *One Last Time.* New York: Berkley Books, 1998. p. 96-99.

9.) Rodegast, Pat and Stanton, Judith. *Emmanuel's Book.* Weston, CT: Friends' Press, 1985. p. ix, 169-171.

10.) Montgomery, Ruth. *A World Beyond.* New York: Fawcett Crest, 1971. p. 12-13.

11.) Freeman, Sidney. *Life After Death,* p. 214-215.

12.) Ibid. p. 199-201.

13.) Ibid. p. 182-183.

14.) Ibid. p. 105-116.

15.) Ibid. p. 179-181.

16.) *Sightings: The Ghost Report.* Documentary from Paramount Pictures. 1995.

17.) Ibid.

18.) Martin and Romanowski, *We Are Not Forgotten,* p. 275.

Evidence Category #6: Input from Religions and Spirituality

1.) Campbell, Joseph and Toms, Michael. *An Open Life.* New York: Harper & Row, 1989. p.64, 52.

2.) Newton, Michael. *Destiny of Souls.* St. Paul, MN: Llewellyn, 2000. p. 245-248.

3.) *U.S. News and World Report* March 25, 1991. p.63.

4.) Douglas-Klotz and Pitstick, The Best of "Soul-utions", 2000.

5.) Borg, Marcus. AP article on the "God at 2000 Conference" in Oregon.

6.) Fox, *Natural Grace,* p. 82, 85, 98.

7.) Dyer, Wayne. *Wisdom of the Ages.* New York: Harper-Collins, 1998. p. 32.

8.) Campbell and Toms, *An Open Life,* p. 55-56, 64-65, and 88.

9.) Moses, Jeffrey. *Oneness: Great Principles Shared by All Religions.* New York: Fawcett Columbine, 1989. p. 24-25.

10.) Burnham, Sophy, *Angel Letters,* p. 125.

11.) Satchidananda, Swami. *To Know Your Self.* Buckingham, VA: Integral Yoga Publications, 1988. p. 47.

12.) Douglas-Klotz, Neil. *Prayers of the Cosmos.* New York: HarperCollins, 1994. p. 12-16.

13.) James, William, *The Varieties of Religious Experience,* p. 320-322.

14.) Errico, Rocco. *Let There Be Light: The Seven Keys.* Marina del Ray, CA: Devorss & Company, 1974. p. 141-142.

15.) Campbell and Toms, *An Open Life,* p. 57.

16.) Douglas-Klotz, Neil, *Prayers Of The Cosmos,* p. 14.

17.) Douglas-Klotz and Pitstick, *The Best of "Soul-utions"*

18.) from "Introduction to Unitarian-Universalism" pamphlet

19.) Miles, Jack. *God: A Biography.* New York: Vintage Books, 1975. p. 6, 9.

20.) Harmon, Willis. *Global Mind Change.* Indianapolis, IN: Knowledge Systems, 1988. p.83.

21.) Douglas-Klotz, *Prayers Of The Cosmos,* p. 1-2, 7

22.) Harner, Michael. *The Way of the Shaman.* Harper & Row: New York, 1980. p. xvii.

23.) Epictetus, *Discourses.*

24.) Armstrong, Karen. *A History Of God.* New York: Ballantine, 1993. p.104, 319.

25.) Campbell and Toms, *An Open Life,* p. 45, 82-83, 60-61.

26.) Smith, Huston. *The World's Religions.* New York: HarperCollins, 1991. p. 5.

Evidence Category #7: Perinatal Experiences

1.) Ring and Cooper, *Mindsight,* p.182.

2.) Wade, *Changes of Mind,* p. 52.

3.) Hallett, Elisabeth. *Soul Trek: Meeting Our Children on the Way to Birth.* Hamilton MT: Light Hearts Publishing, 1995.

4.) Chamberlain, David. *Babies Remember Birth.* Los Angeles: Tarcher, 1988. p. 103-104,106, 120.

5.) Bongard, Jerry. *The Near Birth Experience: A Journey to the Center of Self.* New York: Marlowe and Company, 2000

6.) Grof, Stan. *Beyond the Brain.* Albany, NY: State Univ. of New York Press, 1985. p. 39.

7.) Chamberlain, David. *The Mind of Your Newborn Baby.* Berkeley: North Atlantic Books, 1998. p. 157.

8.) Chamberlain, *Babies Remember Birth,* p.187-188.

9.) Cheek, D. B. (1992.) Are telepathy, clairvoyance and "hearing" possible in utero? *Pre- and Peri-Natal Psychology Journal* 7(2). p.130.

10.) Chamberlain, D.B. (1990). The expanding boundaries of memory. *Pre- and Peri-Natal Psychology Journal* 4(3): 171-189.

11.) Hinze, Sarah. *Coming From the Light: Spiritual Accounts of Life Before Life.* New York: Pocket Books, 1997.

12.) Wade, *Changes of Mind,* p.1, 31-32, 249-250.

Evidence Category #8: Reincarnation Evidence

1.) Schachter-Shalomi, Salman. (Interview with William Elliott.) *Tying Rocks To Clouds.* New York: Doubleday, 1996. p. 180.

2.) Raphael, Simcha Paull. *Jewish* Views *of the Afterlife.* Northvale, NJ: Jason Aronson, 1994. p. 28, 314.

3.) Woolger, Roger. *Other Lives, Other Selves.* New York: Bantam Books, 1987. p. 275, 280.

4.) Weatherhead, Leslie. *The Case for Reincarnation.* Surrey, England: M.C. Peto, 1966.

5.) Freeman, James. *The Case for Reincarnation.* Unity Village, MO: Unity Books, 1986. p. 7.

6.) Weiss, Brian. *Many Lives, Many Masters.* New York: Simon & Schuster, 1988. p. 35.

7.) Woolger, *Other Lives, Other Selves,* p. xviii.

8.) Binder, Bettye and Hogshire, James. *Fifty Amazing Stories of People Who Have Lived Before.* Boca Raton, FL: Globe, 1992. p. 8.

9.) Freeman, *The Case for Reincarnation,* p. 46.

10.) Chopra, Deepak. *How To Know God.* Harmony Books, New York. 2000. p. 234.

11.) Head, Joseph and Cranston, Sylvia. *Reincarnation: The Phoenix Fire Mystery.* Pasadena, CA: Theosophical University Press, 1994. p. 401-402.

12.) Lenz, Frederick. *Lifetimes.* New York: Ballantine Books, 1979. p. 37.

13.) Holzer, Hans. *The Secret of Healing.* Hillsboro, OR: Beyond Words, 1995. p 81.

14.) Newton, Michael. *Journey of Souls.* p. 2.

15.) Bowman, Carol. *Return From Heaven.* New York: HarperCollins, 2001. p. 36-37.

16.) Semkiw, Walter. *Return of the Revolutionaries.* Charlottesville, VA: Hampton Roads. 2002.

17.) Fiore, Edith. *You Have Been Here Before*. New York: Ballantine Books, 1978, p. 239.

18.) Weiss, *Messages From The Masters*, p. 171-173.

19.) Wambach, Helen. *Reliving Past Lives: The Evidence Under Hypnosis*. New York: Harper & Row. 1978. p. 111-146.

20.) Whitton, Joel and Fisher, Joe. *Life Between Life*. Garden City, NY: Doubleday, 1986. p. 144-156.

21.) Weiss, *Messages From The Masters*, p. 82-85.

22.) Cockell, Jenny. *Across Time and Death*. New York: Simon & Schuster, 1993.

23.) Weiss, *Messages From The Masters*, p. 46.

24.) Bowman, *Children's Past Lives*, p. 147, 332-333.

25.) Wade, *Changes of Mind*, p. 111.

26.) Algeo, John. *Reincarnation: The Evidence* (magazine article in *The Quest*) March-April 2001, p. 44-50.

27.) Bowman, *Return from Heaven*, p. 124.

28.) Stevenson, *Where Reincarnation and Biology Intersect*, p.112-113.

Evidence Category #9: Firsthand Experience and Inner Knowing

1.) Swedenborg, Emanuel. *Concerning Divine Love & Wisdom*.

2.) Dyer and Pitstick, *The Best of "Soul-utions"*, 2000.

3.) Wilber, Ken. *No Boundary*. Boulder: Shambhala, 1985. p. 143.

4.) *Mundaka Upanishad*. I, 2.2.

5.) *Bhagavad*-Gita. 2:55a.

6.) Smith, *The World's Religions*, p. 46.

7.) Oyler, *Go Toward The Light*, p.237.

8.) Dyer and Pitstick, *The Best of "Soul-utions"*

9.) Smith, *The World's Religions*, p. 82.

10.) *Vairacchedik.* 32.

11.) James, *The Varieties of Religious Experiences*, p. 323-324.

12.) Dyer, *Wisdom of the Ages*, p. 137.

13.) Dyer and Pitstick, *The Best of "Soul-utions"*

About the Author

Mark Pitstick, M.A., D.C., has over 30 years experience and training in hospitals, mental health centers, pastoral counseling settings, and holistic private practice. His training includes a premedical degree, graduate theology/pastoral counseling studies, masters in clinical psychology, and doctorate in chiropractic.

He was certified in past life regression therapy by Brian Weiss, M.D., and the after-death contact technique by Raymond Moody, M.D.

His books have been endorsed by Drs. Wayne Dyer, Elisabeth Kubler-Ross, Deepak Chopra, Bernie Siegel, Ken Ring, Alan Cohen, and others.

A frequent radio and TV talk show guest, Mark hosted *"Soulutions,"* a nationally syndicated radio show focusing on soul issues and practical spirituality. His audiotape/CD set, *The Best of "Soulutions"*, contains exclusive interviews with world renowned experts on afterlife evidence and soul issues.

Dr. Pitstick facilitates workshops and provides psycho-spiritual counseling across the country. He has been a review editor and regular contributor to many magazines and e-zines. Mark is the director of the Balanced Living Chiropractic Center and uses advanced holistic health care techniques.

ORDER and CONTACT INFORMATION

Mark Pitstick, MA, DC

P.O. Box 1604 • Chillicothe, OH 45601

mark@soulproof.com email

740-775-2189 • 740-774-4778 fax

www.soulproof.com

Printed in the United States
78628LV00004B/38